A LANDSCAPE REVEALED

10,000 Years on a Chalkland Farm

Martin Green

with a contribution by Michael J. Allen

TEMPUS

First published 2000

PUBLISHED IN THE UNITED KINGDOM BY:

Tempus Publishing Ltd
The Mill, Brimscombe Port
Stroud, Gloucestershire GL5 2QG

PUBLISHED IN THE UNITED STATES OF AMERICA BY:

Arcadia Publishing Inc.
A division of Tempus Publishing Inc.
2 Cumberland Street
Charleston, SC 29401

Tempus books are available in France, Germany and Belgium
from the following addresses:

Tempus Publishing Group	Tempus Publishing Group	Tempus Publishing Group
21 Avenue de la République	Gustav-Adolf-Straße 3	Place de L'Alma 4/5
37300 Joué-lès-Tours	99084 Erfurt	1200 Brussels
FRANCE	GERMANY	BELGIUM

British Library Cataloguing in Publication Data.
A catalogue record for this book is available from the British Library.

ISBN 0 7524 1490 9

Typesetting and origination by Tempus Publishing.
PRINTED AND BOUND IN GREAT BRITAIN.

Contents

Acknowledgements

Other than to the sources of the photographs and illustrations which are acknowledged in the captions, the writer is grateful to the following: for comments on earlier drafts I am particularly indebted to Nick Barton and my wife Karin; Mike Allen not only produced chapter 3 but has been a source of help and inspiration in many other ways; John Arnold for access and discussion of his fieldwalking results, including figures 13 and 39.

For help in the field I am grateful to all those who have wielded trowel and shovel over the years, in particular Jim Russell, Paul Kitching, John and Della Day and Dave Bennett. The principal illustrator was Nick Griffiths, with Dave Bennett (reconstructions) and Joanna Richards (lithics). Dave Cousins produced additional photography at short notice. Microlight pilots Mervyn Hinge and Cliff Sims gave me opportunities to view the area from a different perspective. For help in other ways I would like to thank Thomas Blacklock, Steve Burrow, Keith Faxon, Dave Field, Charly French, Julie Gardiner, Peter Hawes, Frances Healy, Andy Lawson, Barry Lewis, Roger Mercer, Tim Schadla-Hall, Mick Tizzard, Dave Webb and Ian West. Richard Bradley has been a constant source of encouragement and practical help. Finally to all those farmers and landowners who have readily given access to their land for my researches — thank you.

Dedicated to the memory of my father
Tom Green 1909-99 who kindled the flame

Foreword

G.K. Chesterton once wrote that if you look at something ninety-nine times you are perfectly safe. But if you look at it again, you are in terrible danger of seeing it for the first time. He should have been an archaeologist!

Cranborne Chase must be one of the most thoroughly investigated regions in British archaeology. It is where General Pitt Rivers laid down the principles of modern excavation and it has been studied in two separate volumes by the former Royal Commission and in two more by a team who worked there in the late 1970s and early '80s. So much remained to be found that this work hardly skimmed the surface. Our knowledge of that region has been transformed by the work of one man. Working there year after year, often on his own, Martin Green has built up a picture of the ancient landscape that can hardly be matched anywhere else in the British Isles.

Of course, he is fortunate in living and working in an exceptionally rich area (the Dorset Cursus, one of the largest monuments built in the Neolithic period, actually crosses his farm) and that may be why some of the sites he describes here are so unusual. But if he makes a speciality of finding new kinds of monument, Martin has far more than good luck on his side. He is an unusually patient and careful observer. I doubt whether he misses anything, from a flint flake to a Roman villa, and his persistence has been rewarded many times over. He works in one of the best-known and best-investigated areas in British archaeology, yet his research has allowed us to see it with new eyes.

The story he has to tell is an exceptionally interesting one in which the development of Cranborne Chase is interwoven with an account of his own fieldwork. It begins with chance discoveries that could have been made on any part of the chalk of southern England and it ends with a unique programme of research, in which Martin plays a pivotal role, involving no fewer than five universities and one of the major field units. There are few, if any, projects that have shown a greater staying power, yet its results continue to surprise us year after year. It makes a nonsense of the distinction between amateur and professional that has done so much to damage archaeology in this country. Martin must be the most professional amateur in Britain, but his work is so important that the term is simply insufficient. His achievement is unique, and this book shows us why.

Richard Bradley

The illustrations

Text figures

(All photographs are by the author and all drawings by Nick Griffiths unless otherwise stated)

Colour plates

Cover photo
      The Dorset Cursus crossing Down Farm. Fir Tree Field, where a number of excavations
      have taken place, can be seen at the top

Preface

I was raised on an isolated farm in the middle of Cranborne Chase **(1)** where I still live. Born into a long line of farmers it was natural for me to continue in the family tradition. However, I discovered at an early age my true vocation was in trying to unravel the mysterious past which lay all around me. With such farm field names as Cursus Field and Gussage Down Field, I could not have been in a better place to start my quest **(2)**. As a boy I was impressed by the fossils and flint implements my father occasionally found during his work on the farm and it was not long before I was wandering the fields in search of such 'treasures'. I soon started to find the most common local fossils — sea urchins known locally as 'shepherd's crowns' — but flint implements were harder to recognise in fields full of naturally shattered flints. Much consultation at local museums was needed before a discerning eye was developed. Later I was to find my first piece of Roman pottery within yards of our home. On learning that it was almost 2000 years old, I assumed it must be very fragile and duly varnished it. About this time I interested a school friend in my hobby and together we cycled around the area trespassing in ploughed

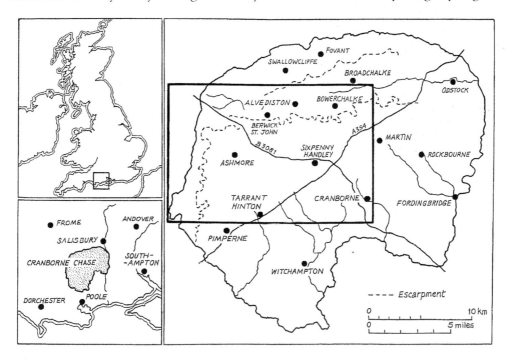

1   Location map of Cranborne Chase with the main study area highlighted

2   *Vertical aerial photograph of Down Farm taken in 1972. The Dorset Cursus can be seen crossing from bottom left to top right and the Ackling Dyke obliquely from centre top to bottom. Fir Tree Field lies in the top right hand corner and contains a number of visible sites which were subsequently excavated. The naleds show up at centre right as a series of light and dark blotches.* (Courtesy Dorset County Council)

fields wherever we thought we might find something; we were always much too afraid to ask for permission. Together we used to spend many a Saturday visiting Dorchester or Salisbury museums comparing our finds to those on display and pestering the curators to look at our discoveries. We always came away from these visits with renewed energy to make even greater finds in future. We began to amass a lot of material and we both started our rival museums. During our teens we took part in a number of Ministry excavations and learnt the basics of excavation techniques. My friend Barry subsequently went to university where he gained his degree in archaeology, while I went to work on the family farm and was able to continue my researches in my free time and occasionally at work — many a time have I jumped down from a tractor to rescue a find.

In the 'great drought' of 1976, with the lowering water table exacerbated by the installation of a new water company pumping station, we had mains water connected to the farm. During the digging of the pipe trench a prehistoric ditch was discovered (3). I wanted to know more about this ditch. What was its purpose? What date was it? This chance discovery led me into my own series of excavations which, twenty years on, I am still conducting. Richard Bradley from Reading University heard of this recent research

3   The start of my excavations — a Bronze Age ditch revealed in a trench dug to lay a water main during the 'great drought' of 1976

and paid me a visit. He informed me of his and colleague John Barrett's plan to re-examine one of Pitt Rivers' excavations and to reassess the prehistory of the area in the light of current knowledge. As my own work was covering similar ground it was suggested that we should combine our resources and work on a joint reappraisal of the area. This was how the Cranborne Chase project was born. Work in the field continued until 1984 including the completion of eight separate excavations, three quarters of which took place on Down Farm. The following five years concentrated on analysis and synthesis, culminating in the publication of two volumes on the work (Barrett et al 1991, 1991a). Since the completion of the project my research continues, and will no doubt do so for as long as I am able. My current work in the area in partnership with Mike Allen is concentrating on the ancient environment, which we regard as phase II of the Cranborne Chase Project (see chapter 3). In tandem with our work, further projects include detailed work on ancient soils by Charly French of Cambridge University and investigation of the Upper Paleolithic site at Deer Park Farm by Nick Barton of Oxford Brookes (see chapter 1). Once again a large part of these studies are based within the Down Farm landscape.

The published work of the project to date, when combined with the most recent work on the area by the Royal Commission of Historical Monuments (Bowen 1991), brings Cranborne Chase once again to the forefront of archaeological landscape studies within Britain. With the future publication of the current projects the Down Farm area will become the most studied piece of ancient chalk downland landscape within Western Europe.

It seems only fitting that a hundred years on from the pioneering work of Pitt Rivers within Cranborne Chase, which laid so solid a foundation for the scientific study of archaeology in the twentieth century, we end the century with a review of what has been achieved in the area since.

For archaeology to reach a wider public was one of the General's main aims and I hope this book successfully continues that process.

Note on radiocarbon dates

Most radiocarbon results (BP) in the strictly archaeological timescale are calibrated to ensure parity with calendar dates. These are cal BC.

Where results are before about 6000 cal BC calibration is more difficult and many dates of late glacial and earlier epochs are recorded in line with palaeo-geographical timescales. These are recorded as years BP (ie. before present – 1950; they are uncalibrated).

The late Upper Palaeolithic and Mesolithic periods occur where calibration is not readily comparable, yet comparison with archaeological (cal BC) dates is required. Here (especially table 2), BC dates are presented. These are the uncalibrated results (BP), minus 1950, to give BC.

Introduction

The earliest parts of the present farmstead date to the beginning of the nineteenth century. Remarkably, the farm itself is mentioned, although not by name, by the antiquarian Sir Richard Colt Hoare in his famous two-volume work on Ancient Wiltshire. In describing the course of the Dorset Cursus to the east of Gussage Cow Down, he states: 'How often have I reviewed with fresh delight this truly interesting ground, and with what sincere regret, on revisiting this spot in the autumn of 1817, did I notice the encroachments of the plough on this memorable, and till lately, well preserved monument of early antiquity. A new farm has been created in the valley, and the lines of the Cursus cut across and levelled'. Naturally, it is exciting to find the farm mentioned in such a classic of antiquarian literature even though the context could have been more auspicious.

Down Farm occupies part of a broad downland valley, one of several which cross an area of chalk upland known as Cranborne Chase. Gently rising from the south-east near Wimborne, the downlands gradually increase in elevation until the dizzy heights of the escarpment crowned by the summit of Win Green at 277m (910ft). The eastern boundary overlaps the edge of the Hampshire basin where Tertiary deposits of sands and gravels clothe the chalk. Below the escarpment to the west and north lie older geological formations which comprise the vales of Blackmoor and Wardour. Cranborne Chase is broadly bounded by water on its eastern and southern sides by the rivers Avon and Stour respectively, with tributaries of these forming the boundaries to the west and north. Dissecting the area are a number of south-easterly flowing streams such as the Allen in whose valley Down Farm lies (4). These streams feed the two great rivers which eventually discharge their waters into the English Channel at Christchurch harbour near Bournemouth. Once, these streams were transformed into raging torrents by the unleashing of meltwater trapped by frost and ice around the periphery of the glaciers at the end of the last Ice Age, some 10-20,000 years ago. Such torrents would erode and transport vast quantities of chalk previously weakened by being frozen to considerable depths. Evidence of such great erosion can best be seen in the magnificent sculpted dry valleys on the northern escarpment (5). This eroded material would be transported down the streams, some partly to fill the valleys with deposits known as 'coombe rock', the rest to find its way out to sea. On Down Farm some of this material built up around frozen springs then present in the valley floor, creating a strange contorted landscape. These proved to be the first examples of 'naleds', as the mounds and hollows are known, to have been found in Britain outside East Anglia (Catt et al 1980). A section dug through one small mound revealed over 4 metres of re-deposited chalky gravels (6). A drive down our farm lane reveals a series of undulations as the naleds are crossed.

Excess water released at this time would have eroded its way into fissures and other

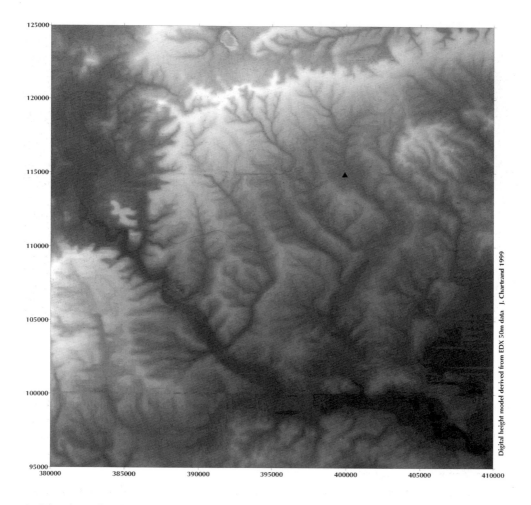

Digital height model derived from EDX 50m data   J. Chartrand 1999

4   *The physical outline of Cranborne Chase with Down Farm pinpointed.* (Courtesy Bournemouth University)

weaknesses in the chalk creating deep holes, caverns and tunnel valleys within the chalk bedrock. A collapsed example of the latter was excavated in Fir Tree Field (see chapter 3) and another (proven by augering) lies just outside the entrance to a small henge monument at Pentridge *(see* **24)**. Close to the northern end of Down Farm is the partially infilled remains of an example so large it is known as 'Endless Pit' *(see* **50)** and has given its name to the crossroads at this point. On a flight last year I observed a semi-circular crop mark partly enclosing the pit, suggesting that this and other such natural features were regarded as sacred openings into 'mother earth', perhaps where rites of initiation, placation and communication could take place. Masses of flint washed away with the chalk would also move downstream to build up further deposits of gravel where the streams slackened their pace. Just such deposits cover much of Down Farm. Eroded clay with flints soils remain on parts of the downs particularly to the north, and today it is on these

5   Aerial view looking east along the northern edge of the escarpment from Win Green

areas that the bulk of the existing woodland remains. Some pockets of clay with flints do occur farther south, however, including on Down Farm, giving it a surprising variety of geology and soils in an area of limited geological variability. Along the south-eastern edge, isolated pockets of Reading beds sands, clay and gravel occur before the main thrust of the Tertiary deposits are reached.

Geology and topography have had a profound effect on man's use of the land once the area was initially exploited at the end of the last Ice Age. As we shall see, the first hunter-gatherer groups chose particular locations based on availability of resources such as water and flint combined with a closeness to the greatest range of habitats available in the shortest distance. The first farming communities, still partly reliant on hunting, exploited these same areas but also expanded onto the lighter soils more suitable for cultivation. These pioneer farmers raised the first earthworks, indelible markers proclaiming the communities' presence. Earthworks such as these focused attention on specific locations that may already have had a long history as important places. Expanding populations towards the end of the Neolithic and beginning of the Bronze Age saw the area develop into a 'sacred landscape' full of social and cultural meaning. Existing special locations were further embellished and new areas were demarcated by the construction of literally hundreds of burial and ritual monuments. Towards the end of the Bronze Age this world of symbolic meaning begins to break down and we start to see a new landscape emerge based on an increasingly ordered system of land division and management. This system culminates in the succeeding Iron Age when the land appears to be populated to capacity and ritual foci and activity concentrates within the settlements.

6 *Trench through periglacial naled on Down Farm 1976*

   This successful system continues throughout the Roman occupation with surpluses used to swell Imperial coffers. Some families, perhaps descended from tribal leaders, become wealthy and are able to build sumptuous villa complexes. This economic prosperity and social order becomes increasingly threatened during the fourth century by cross-channel raiders and starts to break down in the fifth century with the removal of the legions. The incoming Saxons eventually breach Bokerley Dyke and start to position their dwellings in new river valley locations. The old downland settlements, many continuously occupied for over a thousand years, are gradually deserted as the foundations of our present-day villages and settlements are laid.

   We shall see in the unfolding chapters that the authors' original researches reveal a land scarred with meaning. The landscape of Down Farm is ingrained with these changes, and presents in microcosm what was happening in this most special area of Cranborne Chase.

1 Beginnings:
evidence of the
hunter-gatherers

The Old Stone Age or Palaeolithic 500,000-10,000 BC

Only a few finds of this vast period have been made on Cranborne Chase if one excludes the flints found on the extreme borders of the area. These border finds include a few from close to the Stour at Sturminster Marshall, two from Shaftesbury and the large number of flints found on the terraces of the River Avon during gravel extraction north of Ringwood. The author is only aware of four handaxes, the principal tool of the period, being found at any distance away from the borders.

During this long period of time the area was subjected to a variety of extreme conditions during the great Ice Ages. These climatic conditions ranged from extreme cold to Mediterranean warmth. Although glaciers did not come as far south as Cranborne Chase, permafrost kept the area in its icy grip and the landscape would have been similar to Arctic tundra. Large hairy herbivores would have wandered over the area such as mammoths, reindeer and woolly rhinoceros. During periods of thaw massive meltwaters would re-arrange the landscape by moving huge amounts of frost weakened chalk which would be deposited lower down the valleys altering the courses of the river systems. In these much longer warmer periods known as interglacials temperatures were sometimes even higher than today's and conditions would have been more suitable for occupation than the colder glacial periods. Bone remains show that elephants, rhinos, lions and even hippopotamus thrived in these periods when Britain was still attached to the mainland of Europe. A sand-filled fissure dating to this period, found at Dewlish just north of Dorchester, contained masses of elephant bones when excavated in the last century (Reid 1915). A similar fissure discovered during the construction of the Handley Hill roundabout in 1976 contained highly polished pebbles but no animal bones in the section excavated. In these warmer periods human groups followed the animals across into Britain and hunted them. They left their butchery tools at campsites usually near rivers, which have subsequently changed course and moved these tools downstream into banks of gravel, to be unearthed again during gravel extraction.

However, a few were dropped away from the main rivers and it is these few finds which prove Palaeolithic peoples hunted the Chase hundreds of thousands of years ago. One handaxe of a crudely flaked form found at Moor Crichel probably dates to the earlier part of the period, anywhere between 500,000-350,000 years ago, and another from Brockington Beeches of Acheulian form was probably made around 350,000-200,000 years ago. Two further finely made handaxes found on Handley Common (**7**) and Middle Chase Farm date to the Middle Palaeolithic and are of Mousterian type. These were made by people known

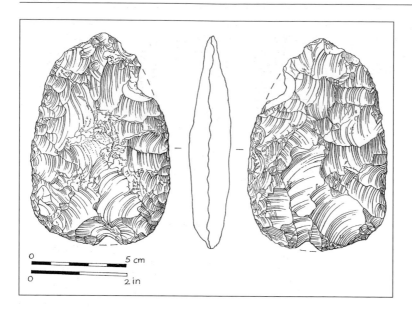

7   *Mousterian 'biface' found on Handley Common* (J.Richards)

as Neanderthals whose hunting range extended into Britain, probably after a warming of the last glacial period around 60,000 BC.

By about 35,000 BC evidence reveals the arrival of new human groups with essentially modern physical characteristics who produced flint industries of fundamentally different type. The arrival of these groups marks the beginning of the period known as the Upper Palaeolithic. Handaxes and flake tools were abandoned in favour of a new range of tools principally produced from blades — long parallel-sided flakes at least three times longer than their breadth. This technological advance seems to be associated with increased evidence for the hafting of bone and flint artefacts. A series of backed blades, for instance, could be set into a slotted handle and fixed with natural resin to form a long cutting edge. Not only was this more efficient than a handaxe but it could also be repaired almost indefinitely with the replacement of individual blades when blunted or damaged. The range of tool forms produced from these blades is also wider and reveals greater emphasis on the working of wood, bone, antler and ivory. The period is also demarcated by the first appearance of complex art, a few small examples of which have been found in Britain.

The Upper Palaeolithic is further sub-divided into earlier and later phases marked by changes in both flint technology and climate. In Britain there is a major hiatus between these two phases caused by a very cold period which made Britain uninhabitable for about six thousand years after 18,000 BC. At the end of this phase rare evidence starts to appear of recolonisation by hunter-gatherer groups including a site revealed on Cranborne Chase.

Deer Park Farm

This site near Wimborne St Giles is perched on a knoll close to a spring at the junction between the chalklands and the start of the Tertiary deposits of the Hampshire basin. Only just located on the edge of the Reading beds clay it was revealed as a discrete scatter of worked flint during part of the author's fieldwalking programme (Green et al 1998). At the time of writing around 1000 worked flints have been collected. These consist almost entirely of

8 *Upper Palaeolithic core 1, blades 2-4 and end scraper 5, from Deer Park Farm* (J.Richards)

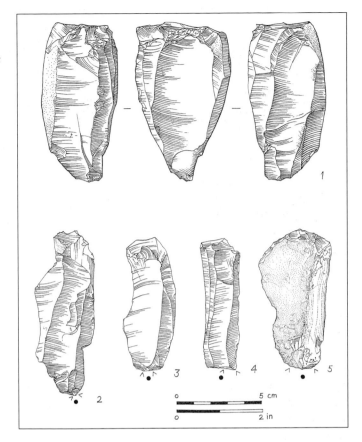

unmodified flakes and blades and the resulting cores from which they were struck **(8)**. The flint used was collected from immediately accessible clay deposits that even today yield occasional nodules of high quality. Careful searching would have been required to locate this material with perhaps the finished products being taken off site. However, numbers of burnt artefacts suggested some form of occupation, which was confirmed by a very small excavation **(9)**. A layer 20cm thick below the ploughsoil was revealed to contain scraps of charcoal with burnt artefacts.

Insufficient charcoal was recovered for a radiocarbon date but a burnt flint artifact was submitted for thermoluminescence dating which produced a date of 10,740±1200BP. This date spans the Upper Palaeolithic/Early Mesolithic transition but the typology of the artefacts suggests the date would be nearer the earlier end of the spectrum. Assemblages of this date from Britain are very rare and consistently produce tool components of less than 2%, fitting the Deer Park Farm assemblage very well. It seems that these groups were highly mobile and sites like this may represent very short episodes, perhaps as little as a few hours, when the group stopped, rested, ate and replenished their flint tool kit, leaving only the waste behind.

This fortunate discovery provides us with a glimpse of one of the very small bands of hunters exploiting the birch forest present in southern Britain at this time. However, it is not until the succeeding Mesolithic period that we get clear evidence for more sustained occupation.

9   *Excavations uncovering further finds at the Deer Park Farm Upper Palaeolithic site* (P. Hawes)

The Middle Stone Age or Mesolithic 10,000-4,000 BC

With the final retreat of ice sheets from upland Britain about 10,000 years ago the climate gradually became warmer and forest, birch and pine at first, started to clothe the open landscape. The animals of the tundra retreated north with the ice and into the establishing forests came aurochs (large wild cattle), red deer, wild boar, bear, wolf and beaver. New hunters came too and were already adept at hunting these animals in their wooded environment. A gradual warming during this period and subsequent rise in sea level caused the English Channel to be formed around 5400 BC, forcing people to take to boats to reach this country. This warming up saw the gradual replacement of the birch and pine forests by mixed oak forest. Mesolithic people would have used the major rivers as highways to penetrate the densely forested hinterland and it was probably by the Stour and its tributaries that they reached Cranborne Chase and Down Farm. These people worked flint in a distinctive way by flaking large numbers of long, narrow and very thin blades from carefully prepared cores. Only the blades of suitable dimensions and ideal thickness were selected for further modification into small arrow tips and barbs known as microliths **(10)**. When mounted in arrow shafts these small flint points have been shown by experiment to be highly effective hunting weapons (Barton and Bergman 1982). Significant numbers of them have been found with distinctive damage at the tip. Exact replication of these fractures has been achieved through experiments where arrows tipped with microliths were shot into animal carcasses.

The resulting flint waste produced from the manufacture of microliths is often extensive and is relatively easy to locate through fieldwalking on ploughed land. A thorough survey can thus reveal many of the former habitation areas of these skilful

10 Middle Stone Age microlithic flint industries

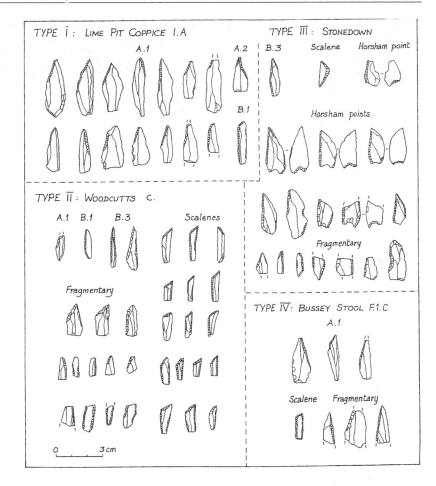

TYPE Ī : LIME PIT COPPICE I.A

TYPE ĪĪĪ : STONEDOWN

TYPE ĪĪ : WOODCUTTS C.

TYPE ĪV : BUSSEY STOOL F.1.C

hunters. On Cranborne Chase a striking distribution pattern for these sites has emerged as shown by the map **(11)**. Those findspots not in the river valleys are all located close to the springheads which emerge at the bottom of the low chalk hills. They are also mainly sited on superficial deposits of clay with flints and Reading beds (sandy soil with pebbles above clay) overlying the chalk (Arnold et al 1988). The marked preference shown by humans for these soils suggests that there were important reasons why they were located in such places. We know that the best quality flint in the area, vital to Stone Age hunters, is to be found in these deposits where it has been kept damp, reasonably fresh and free from frost damage. Also these soils would have produced a different and wider range of plant resources especially near the boundary with the chalk where different edge-adapted species would occur. The chalk itself would be more lightly forested with little undergrowth and consequently more suitable for hunting. The three sites on the Greensand below the chalk escarpment are next to major springs and are ideally situated either to exploit the chalk of Cranborne Chase or the older formations provided by the vales of Blackmoor and Wardour. Campsites were therefore placed in the optimum position to exploit the widest range of ecological resources available within the shortest possible distance, as well as being on the best flint source and close to water. The changing

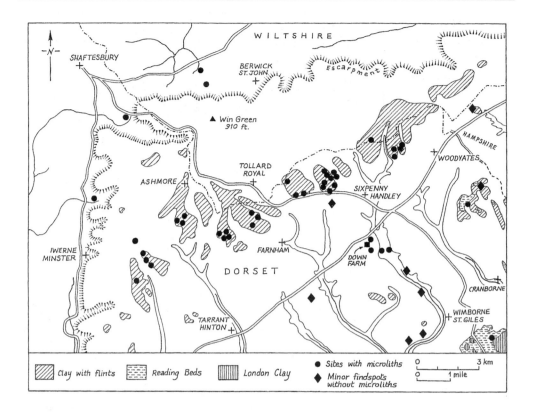

11 The distribution of Mesolithic sites on Cranborne Chase

climate and environment during this period is reflected in the changing tool kit. The most distinctive flint of the period is the microlith which tipped and barbed the hunting arrows. Generally they tend to be fairly large and of simple design at the beginning of the period, but progressively get smaller and more elaborate towards the end. These changes are very useful from a chronological point of view and show that in our area the bulk of the activity took place towards the middle and latter end of the Mesolithic period.

Three distinctive types of sites appear to be represented here. Type I sites are dominated by simple obliquely worked microliths with a few of geometric form. Type II sites consist of a large percentage (at least one third) of scalene triangles and type III sites have a significant proportion of microliths known as Horsham or hollow based points. A fourth possible group, IV, is provided by sites which have only produced non-geometric microliths, although it is likely that the geometric forms, more difficult to find on ploughed land because of their small size, have generally evaded detection so far (*see* **10** for microlith groups). The three or four types of site probably represent different periods of exploitation within the Chase. Occasionally it is possible to suggest, following the work of Mellars (1976), that some sites represent hunting camps and others were probably base camps. Sites which have high proportions of microliths (over 85%, Mellars group A) are more likely to be hunting camps, whilst those with higher percentages (lower than 85%

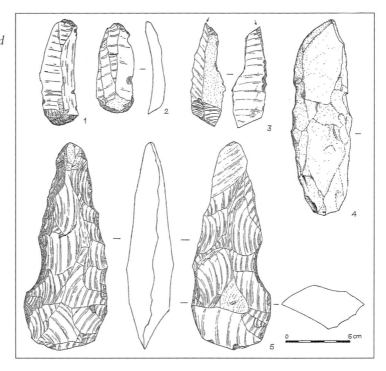

12 Mesolithic larger stone artefacts — end scrapers 1-2, burin 3, pick made from Portland limestone/chert 4, and tranchet axe 5. (B. Lewis)

and usually between 30-60%) of other 'essential' tools (scrapers, burins, saws and axes **(12)**, Mellars group B) were almost certainly occupied for longer periods with a much wider range of activities taking place. A much rarer group, C, produces scrapers in excess of 80%. Eight Cranborne Chase sites, which have produced at least 50 tools of the five categories already mentioned, have been subject to analysis. Table 1a reveals only one site of category A, that of Cann Common on the Upper Greensand. Interestingly enough the much larger site of Rowberry, although in group B, has the next highest percentage of microliths and is also located on Upper Greensand, which probably indicates the better hunting terrain provided by the less heavily forested formation. This site is particularly large, comprising an area in excess of some 700 x 200m situated around a major spring. Careful fieldwork by John Arnold has revealed four main areas within the spread, which are all dominated by microliths of geometric form, particularly scalene triangles. A site of this magnitude in such a favourable location almost certainly evolved through repeated, probably seasonal, occupation. Such accumulations would have developed over a very long period of time, perhaps even millennia.

The remaining sites all fall within group B and can therefore be regarded as base camps although differing considerably in their length of occupation. Occasionally where fieldwork has been sufficiently intense it is even possible to isolate clusters of artefacts within larger spreads of material. The site of Iwerne Minster, for example, exhibits this clustering (J.Arnold *pers.comm*) but analysis has not been attempted due to earlier work. Originally discovered by a local schoolmaster (Summers 1941), the dense flint scatter was subjected to intense collecting with some excavation. Inevitably the remaining material will be much depleted and likely to be unrepresentative in certain categories.

Interestingly this site and that of Rowberry represent the two richest concentrations on the Chase and both share positions close to the chalk escarpment edge near to springs feeding river systems which cross the low lying vales. However, the most useful site for study is Handley Common where detailed survey work over many years has been undertaken by John Arnold **(13)**. Thirteen separate clusters (see Table 1b) have been revealed but it is site 8/9/10 which is particularly interesting. Here a group of six separate nuclei have been isolated in a much larger overall spread. The spatial patterning reveals considerable complexity which may represent different activity areas.

Table 1a

	Microliths & Camp tools	Microlith Percentage	Camp tool Percentage	Dominant Microlith Percentage*	Site Group	Geology	M'rs Gp
Lime Pit Coppice I	52	62%	38%	90.9%	I/IV	CWF	B
Woodcutts C	51	64.7%	35.3%	85%	II	CWF	B
Woodyates B	133	61.6%	38.4%	88.1%	I/IV	CWF	B
St Giles Field	68	41%	59%	95.2%	I/IV	VG	B
Iwerne Minster	648	45.7%	54.3%	79.9%	1	CWF	B
Rowberry	441	74.1%	25.9%	35.6%	II	UGS	B
Cann Common	59	93%	7%	50%	II	UGS	A
Handley Common 8/9/10+	72	36.1%	63.9%	36.4%	I	CWF	B

Table 1b

	Microliths & Camp tools	Microlith Percentage	Camp tool Percentage	Dominant Microlith Percentage*	Site Group	Geology	M'rs Gp
Handley Common 1	9	22.2%	77.8%	100%	I/IV	CWF	B
Handley Common 4	23	43.5%	56.5%	71.4%	I/IV	CWF	B
Handley Common 5	37	45.9%	54.1%	31.2%	III	CWF	B
Handley Common 8/9/1O A	18	62.5%	37.5%	66.6%	II	CWF	B
Handley Common 8/9/1O B	10	10%	90%	?	?	CWF	C
Handley Common 8/9/1O C	16	38.9%	61.1%	42.8%	I	CWF	B
Handley Common 8/9/1O D	17	23.5%	76.5%	100%	I/IV	CWF	B
Handley Common 8/9/10 F	8	25%	75%	100%	I/IV	CWF	B
Handley Common 8/9/1O F	3	66.7%	33.3%	?	?	CWF	B
Handley Common 11 A	10	36.4%	63.6%	100%	I/IV	CWF	B
Handley Common 11/12/13/14	12	8.3%	91.7%	?	?	CWF	C
Handley Common 11/14/15	6	16.7%	83.3%	?	?	CWF	B
Handley Common 23/11	6	16.7%	83.3%	100%	II	CWF	B

★ = Calculated from identifiable microlith totals only ie. fragments not included + = 8/9/10 group assemblages treated as one assemblage

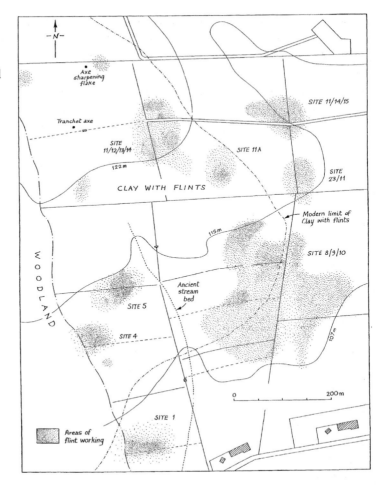

13 Distribution of Mesolithic sites on Handley Common (after John Arnold unpublished)

Cluster B, for instance, reveals a large percentage of scrapers where skin processing may have been taking place, and areas to the south-east of the site produced large amounts of waste suggestive of flint procurement and primary flaking. The range of the dominant microlith percentages indicates some time depth is involved between the clusters but are far from conclusive on this point.

Due to the very small numbers of 'essential' tools recovered from each of the clusters these results must be regarded as highly tentative and have therefore also been amalgamated in Table 1a where the percentages place the site within the balanced base camp category B. Nevertheless, only by detailed survey work of this kind can we hope to gain a better understanding of the complex nature of these sites which are now mostly represented by surface scatters. However, very occasionally stratified sites are discovered which allow us a more intimate view of human activities. Such an example is the site at Downton excavated in the 1950s on the north-eastern edge of the Chase (Higgs 1959).

This carefully excavated site consisted of a well-defined flint working area in excess of 70m squared situated on a gravel terrace just above the flood plain on the east bank of the River Avon. The site was stratified and rested partly upon the natural gravel and upon a

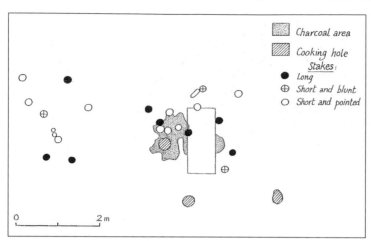

Charcoal area

Cooking hole

Stakes:

● Long

⊕ Short and blunt

○ Short and pointed

0   2 m

14 Mesolithic features recorded at Downton (after Higgs, courtesy Prehistoric Society)

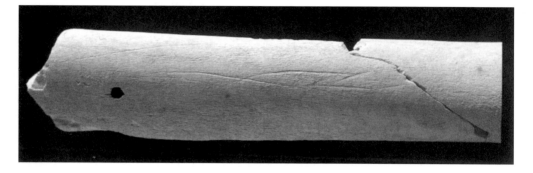

15 Butchered red deer bone from the Fir Tree Field shaft (D.Cousins)

red stoneless silt possibly of wind blown origin. The topsoil contained later Neolithic unpatinated flints but the Mesolithic flints had a light blue surface patina, the colour differences indicating quite a time gap between the two industries. We shall come back to this important question of patina in the next chapter.

Here, the kinds of activity areas already tentatively suggested by the work on Handley Common were well defined. In some cases these areas could be related to features dug into the subsoil. An oval hollow some 3m squared in extent was found to have been dug into the underlying gravel to a maximum depth of half-a-metre (20in). No evidence was discovered in the form of stake or postholes, hearths or spreads of charcoal to suggest that this hollow was actually lived in. However, the largest concentrations of worked flints were found both within it and nearby. Observations made at the time revealed the best-quality flint nodules were found a little way down in the gravel where they were relatively free of frost weaknesses. The excavator concluded that the hollow may have been dug for extracting flint which was knapped on the spot as shown by the higher percentage of cores and waste in this area. Two further areas close to the hollow provided additional evidence for specific activities having taken place. Areas to the south and north, both consisting of about 5% of the chipping floor, yielded over 21% of the scrapers and a third of the saws

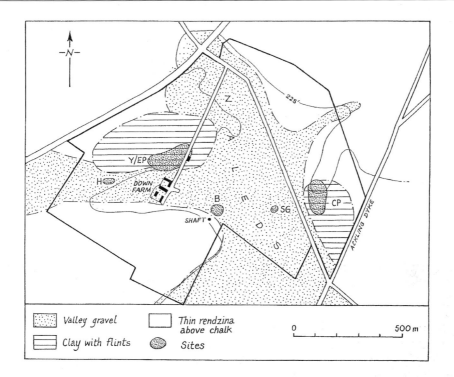

16 Mesolithic sites on Down Farm. H — Home Field, Y/EP — Yard Endless Pit Fields, B — Barn Field, SG — St.Giles Field and CP Chalk Pit Field

respectively. Some 13m to the north of the hollow a clear domestic area was uncovered consisting of two groups of stakeholes **(14)**. One group enclosed a spread of charcoal and two shallow pits described as 'cooking holes' whilst two further pits of this type lay close by. The excavation revealed the traces of a settlement from which a group of hunter-gatherers could exploit the rich environments provided by the river valley itself, the chalklands to the west and the tertiary formations to the east. Stratified sites of this type are very rare and sample excavations undertaken in the area (eg. Lewis & Coleman, 1982) on a number of flint scatters has revealed, with one notable exception, no evidence of undisturbed flintwork surviving the extensive deep ploughing of recent years. The one exception was the site of St Giles Field (Catt et al 1980) on Down Farm where two artefact-rich layers were stratified in the top of a naled mound (see p13). At one end the small trench revealed the lowest layer resting on natural gravel at a depth of 47cm (18in) and at the other to a depth of 70cm (28in). This indicates some disturbance of the gravels during the Mesolithic occupation similar to that found at Downton and the site remains a rare and important resource for future archaeologists.

Remarkable evidence for some of the last hunter-gatherers present in the area was revealed in the 'great shaft' excavated in Fir Tree Field on Down Farm (see chapter 3). Here soils accumulated in an unbroken sequence from 5500-3775BP and contained significant numbers of artefacts and environmental information. The lowest, late

Mesolithic, levels contained worked flint and wild animal bones including a butchered red deer bone **(15)** and two complete young roe deer. A number of dark soil lenses within these levels indicated the presence of forest floor soils within which and interspersed between were significant amounts of charcoal. Amongst other things, the presence of combusted wood suggests the late Mesolithic hunters were using fire to alter their environment. Higher up the sequence dated between 5275 ± 50BP and spanning the Mesolithic/Neolithic transition, further wild animal bones were uncovered including aurochs and a significant group of seven microliths. These were all found in a tight cluster suggesting they had entered the shaft in a hafted state, perhaps as an offering to the gods.

Significantly, five were of narrow rod form characteristic of the latest Mesolithic industries in Britain. During the excavations on the Dorset Cursus in Chalk Pit Field, where a Mesolithic site is also situated, animal bones found in the base of the ditch produced radiocarbon dates in the Mesolithic. One date was in the earlier sixth millennium but the other produced a date of 4340-3690 BC, broadly contemporary with the later Mesolithic sequence in the shaft. It would seem that part of the old land surface had fallen into the Cursus ditch shortly after its excavation, taking with it bones derived from Mesolithic occupation. Environmental information from this level suggested dense woodland which is also most likely derived from a Mesolithic horizon.

The uniquely preserved shaft sequence reflects a well-utilised local land surface and it is perhaps no surprise to reveal a new complex of Mesolithic sites uncovered on Down Farm itself **(16)**. Here the sites are located on superficial deposits in relation to the wide valley which is floored by the naleds. These produce a contorted landscape where water lies even at times today. With a higher water level it is not difficult to imagine the area as a series of natural lakes fed by the river with the naled mounds appearing as a series of 'islands'. Such an environment would have been rich in wildfowl and fish and a focus for larger game, with perhaps denser forest around the margins as indicated by the evidence excavated from the shaft and from Chalk Pit Field. Hunter-gatherer groups would have frequented such a favoured location over many generations. Certainly we have conclusive evidence for a presence in Chalk Pit Field in the early sixth millennium. The stratified site in St Giles Field with its assemblage of non-geometric microliths may well be earlier. The Yard/Endless Pit Field site has produced few microliths but includes rods and numbers of small cores, suggesting a date late in the sequence, perhaps contemporary with the latest levels in the shaft.

The quantity and quality of Mesolithic evidence on Down Farm presents a resource of national significance.

2 Laying the foundations:
the work of General Pitt Rivers

During 1969 my father completed a transaction which added some 66 acres (27 ha) of adjoining land at Thorney Down to our farm. This land belonged to the Pitt Rivers Estate. Thus Down Farm became incidentally associated with a name well known the world over as synonymous with the birth of scientific archaeology. Many years later, in 1992, I was to win the Pitt Rivers Award, presented biannually for the best independent archaeological work undertaken in the country. These connections provide a tangible link to the outstanding work carried out in the area by General Pitt Rivers at the end of the last century. In the course of an afternoon's walk from the farm, I can visit a number of the sites of his pioneering excavations including two barrows just beyond the boundary of Down Farm. It would therefore be inexcusable to continue without a review of the great man's life and work.

Augustus Henry Lane Fox inherited the Rushmore estates in 1880 at the age of 53, and as a condition of the will had to take the name Pitt Rivers. What a small price to pay to become landowner of some 27,000 acres (11,000 ha) centred on Cranborne Chase. For a man of his scientific background it was a godsend as he acknowledges in the introduction to Volume I of his Excavations: 'it almost seemed to me, as if some unseen hand had trained me up to be the possessor of such a property'. His life and works have been thoroughly covered in two recent biographies (Thompson 1977, Bowden 1991), both of which reiterate his right to be regarded as the father of modern scientific archaeology. A brief outline will suffice here.

He was a man at the forefront of scientific thought of the day. A member of the Royal Society he was an enthusiastic supporter of Darwin and numbered Thomas Huxley, Gilbert Spencer and Sir John Lubbock, who was later to become his son-in-law, amongst his friends. He was an avid collector of antiquities, tribal and folk art and artefacts, amassing a vast personal collection of curiosities. When gifted to Oxford University, with the stipulation that the museum in which it was to be housed should bear his name, it became the foundation for the first serious academic study of anthropology in this country. Another requirement was that someone should be appointed to lecture on the collections and this position became the first Chair of Anthropology in a British university. As a military man he was interested in the ancient earthworks and fortifications he observed during his various postings. The first evidence we have for his undertaking of excavations takes place in Ireland in the early 1860s where he dug into several raths (embanked enclosures). He worked later with Canon Greenwell, the indefatigable barrow digger, from whom Pitt Rivers was to say he received his first lessons as an excavator.

Throughout the 1860s and '70s he was busy in fieldwork and excavation on a range

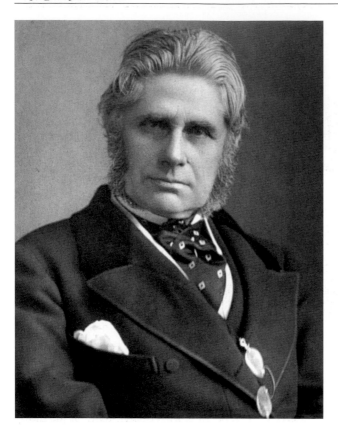

17 General Pitt Rivers

and breadth of sites from the London Roman wall to the Dannewerke, a defensive earthwork crossing the Danish peninsula. His pioneering work on Sussex hillforts led to the discovery and correct interpretation of the pits that underlay the hillfort at Cissbury as Neolithic flint mines. This work had prepared him for his inheritance of a well-preserved archaeological landscape, of which he says: 'I determined to devote the remaining portion of my life chiefly to an examination of the antiquities on my own property'. Within weeks of inheriting the property he was putting this plan into action and was busily digging barrows within Rushmore Park including the Barrow Pleck cemetery (which we shall discuss later). Nationally vast numbers of barrows had been dug into in the preceding hundred years or so and the General was clearly becoming dissatisfied with the rather limited and repetitive information to be gained from the excavation of further examples, stating '... our knowledge of prehistoric and early peoples is derived chiefly from their funeral deposits and for all we know of their mode of life... they might as well have been born dead'. Therefore he soon began his series of pioneering excavations of enclosures and settlement sites which up to this time had largely been ignored.

Due to the seasonality of farm work Pitt Rivers' extended campaigns took place over the autumn and winter period when labourers could be freed from their usual estate tasks. He also employed a number of full-time clerks whose specific duties included site supervision, surveying and the production of records, plans, drawings, models and latterly photographs to enable a detailed report to be prepared on the results from each site. The

18 The Neolithic long barrow, Wor Barrow, under excavation in 1894 (Salisbury & South Wiltshire Museum)

first full season's work took place from Oct 1881 - Feb 1882 and concentrated on the most impressive earthwork close to home: the Iron Age hillfort of Winkelbury overlooking the village of Berwick St John (see chapter 8).

Here he ran into some unexpected difficulties due to local superstition when he removed a dead yew tree, known locally as a 'scrag', from a round barrow during its excavation. The villagers were troubled by his disturbance of the dead and removal of the ancient tree which they believed protected them from malign influences; they were only placated when another dead yew was 'planted' with all due ceremony some time later.

Later that same year, following the acceptance of the Ancient Monuments Act through parliament in October, he was invited to become the first inspector of Ancient Monuments. He enthusiastically accepted and took up his duties in the following January. The work entailed visiting sites that were thought worthy of protection, drawing up accurate plans and models and, most difficult of all, trying to persuade landowners to voluntarily enter into an agreement with the government to ensure their protection.

These visits as inspector generally occupied the summer months and in the winter the excavations continued apace, with the uncovering of the Iron Age and Romano-British settlements of Woodcutts (Oct 1884-Apr 1885 and Oct 1885-Dec 1885) and Rotherley (Oct 1886-Apr 1887). In the autumn of 1887 the first of a series of four sumptuous excavation reports appeared **(colour plate 3)**. The detail contained within these volumes is extraordinary for the time and far in advance of anything that was produced until the work of Sir Mortimer Wheeler (a self-confessed disciple of the General) during the 1930s.

The General published these privately and referred to their rather specialist appeal in the preface to volume III:

'I have frequently been asked to publish these volumes, but after due consideration, I have decided to adhere to my original plan of issuing them privately. There is no demand on the part of the public, for a work of so much detail. Few persons, even amongst those who attend Archaeological meetings, put themselves to the trouble of checking opinions, by sifting the evidence upon which they are based. They prefer to accept results that have become established through the labours of others, more especially if presented to them under the authority of some well-known name. This is a misfortune, no doubt, but it is better than jumping to hasty conclusions upon insufficient data. The results of these excavations have been widely circulated in the proceedings of Archaeological Societies, and in the press. These volumes, containing the evidence upon which the results are based, are intended for workers only, and it appears preferable to retain the privilege of presenting them privately, to those to whom they may perhaps be useful in conducting similar investigations'

He did his best to encourage fellow-workers to record their findings, stating 'a discovery dates only from the time of the record of it, and not from the time of its being found in the soil'. He certainly practised what be preached with only the Roman villa at Iwerne Minster remaining unpublished due to his failing health and eventual death in 1900.

He seems to have had little interest in the traditional pastimes of the landed gentry, preferring fieldwalking to shooting: 'As a healthy exercise it is fully entitled to a place among field sports, and in its objects it is far higher, for whilst the sportsman pushes forward to be in at the death, the goal of the flint hunter is to be in at the birth of a fresh discovery.' This outlook is reflected in a story passed down from the neighbouring Shaftesbury Estate and related to me by a former farm manager, the late John Ironmonger. A shoot had been organised by the Pitt Rivers Estate to which neighbours were invited. During the course of this one of the Generals employees (obviously well trained in archaeological matters), in his duties as a beater for the day, found a flint axe. Much excited by this the General stopped the shoot and organised the beaters in lines to search the area thoroughly, upon which his guests left in disgust!

Certainly many of his labourers became skilled at spotting artefacts whilst about their general farm work. In the collections at Salisbury alongside the excavated material is a large collection of surface finds, mainly larger flint implements collected from the clay with flints areas close to Rushmore and the Larmer Grounds. Interestingly, it was these same areas which became particularly significant during our own fieldwork. On one occasion the General was presented with a splendid chipped Neolithic axe found by a labourer whilst digging a posthole and brought to him as he had heard he was 'curious about stones and such like'.

In tandem with his excavations he was also busily engaged in developing a museum and pleasure grounds. The disposal of his pre-Rushmore collection did not mean an end to his collecting activities, as accounts show that he continued to be an avid buyer of antiquities and ethnographica from London salesrooms and dealers. The desire to educate the public was strong in the Victorian psyche and Pitt Rivers was eager to show his vision of the slow evolutionary progress of mankind and material culture through the medium of displays at his museum near Farnham. These included the fruits of his local excavations and his collecting activities.

In order first to attract visitors he created the nearby pleasure grounds at Larmer Tree, Tollard Royal, now recently re-opened (see Places to Visit). A number of exotic buildings were constructed in the grounds, some purchased from an exhibition at Earls Court. The area was divided into a number of bowers where picnic facilities and amusements were provided. Visitors could listen to the General's brass band, experience a performance at the open-air theatre, or enjoy alternative distractions at the nearby golf links or racecourse. Further attractions included the menagerie of exotic animals at Rushmore and the fine art collections displayed at King John's House, a Medieval building carefully restored by the General. The recorded visitor numbers of 44,417 and 12,611 for the grounds and museum respectively during 1899 shows that this philanthropic gesture was well received. However, not all was rosy at Rushmore as family life appears to have been strained at best. In 1853 the General married Alice Stanley, daughter of Lord Stanley of Alderley. The wedding finally took place after a long and protracted courtship, caused in the main by objections from Alice's family of her suitors' lack of prospects. Even the remotest prospect of the vast inheritance to come would not have been envisaged at that time. The marriage was initially a happy one with Alice usually accompanying her husband on his military postings. Children came thick and fast with six boys and three girls being born over the next thirteen years. However, well before the family moved to Rushmore, the relationship had deteriorated to a state of open hostility. Indeed, Bowden (1991) quotes from a letter written by the General to his wife in the late 1870s in which he states: 'I assure you that for the last four years now you have made my life a perfect curse to me'.

It would seem family life was neither close nor loving. Little interest was shown in his scientific pursuits, with his notoriously mean wife regularly denouncing the extravagances of his excavations. Bertrand Russell, a nephew of Alice, noted her many petty economies which he presumed were 'a result of his expenditure' (ibid. p31). One particular incident he records was 'one of the sons having a tug of war with a lady visitor for the last plate of rice pudding'.

However, the General's account books tell a different story with comparatively modest amounts spent on archaeological investigations that could not have accounted for the extreme economies. In fact he seemed to have taken to estate management with an enthusiastic zeal, producing an annual income of around £20,000. Surviving correspondence in Salisbury Museum reveals that in his dealings with tenants, tradesmen and his agent he could be rude and autocratic, frequently leaving bills unpaid, often to generate prolonged correspondence. In contrast, many of his labourers remembered him with genuine warmth and respect as recorded in a BBC radio broadcast in 1953 (ibid. p12). George Bealing remembered: 'He were'nt no sportin' man for shooting or nothing like that. No, his hobby were road making and tree planting and making ponds. He were a man you could talk to, you know. Nothing proud about 'n'.' Perhaps once again he was

19 Designed by Sir John Evans and struck by Pitt Rivers these medalets were left by him at the sites of his former excavations for future investigators to find. (Courtesy Salisbury & South Wilts Museum)

ahead of his time in anticipating the environmentally conscious times in which we now live. Another employee, Frank Adams from Sixpenny Handley, recalled how anyone could approach the General and talk with him at the Larmer Grounds: 'It was his greatest joy ... to see the people there at Larmer ... enjoying themselves; there was no question about that. That seemed to me to be his one aim — that was to make enjoyment for the other people ... of this neighbourhood.'

This view also seems to have been shared by Hilda Petrie, wife of the famous Egyptologist, when she and her husband visited Rushmore in 1898. Her impressions of the visit were described as 'like spending a day in fairyland' and were set down in a letter to her sister, which has recently come to light (Drower 1994). The couple were driven from Tisbury, the nearest railway station, and 'before long, we came on to Pitt Rivers' ground, all the gates bright blue with yellow tops, like the covers of his archaeological pamphlets'.

Continuing through the park, 'the place was full of deer, the red, fallow, Formosa and Japanese deer, very tame, lying by the lodge doors and indisposed to move, and there were black yaks and other animals'. Arriving at the house the distinguished couple were ushered in after an initial frosty reception from Mrs Pitt Rivers. They learnt the General was unwell and in bed, but upon hearing of their arrival he rose whilst they 'were shown round the great palatial house to see treasures' by one of the Generals' assistants whose job was to illustrate artefacts found during his digs. Eventually the General appeared 'a very fine big old man, with straight features and long white hair and bushy beard' and continued the tour, revealing rooms crowded with antiquities. During this tour the General received a telegram with the offer of a Spanish cannon, weighing three quarters

20 The Pottery Room, Farnham Museum

of a ton. He told his secretary to have it sent on approval. The journey of this antique armament, nine miles across the downland by wagon, must have been quite a sight! Whether it made the trip back again is not known. After lunch the couple were driven to the Larmer Grounds 'through miles of park avenues and nut-woods, and across open down of golf-ground, and meadows full of earth-works and circles which he is going to excavate'. A thorough tour ensued with King John's house, Tollard Royal church, the Larmer Grounds and finally the Museum all visited. Describing the latter Hilda wrote it was 'beautifully and simply built, splendidly lighted and arranged, with nothing to distract the attention, and all white-painted' **(20)**. The vivid account of this visit records the extraordinary wealth and diversity of the attractions, principally created and lovingly presented by 'the King of the place'. It is little wonder that despite its isolated location tens of thousands of visitors flocked there during the final years of the last century.

Following the General's death, fierce wrangling broke out among his children over the will including litigation over the future of the Larmer Grounds and Museum. Remaining closed for some time the museum was eventually re-opened by the General's grandson Captain George Pitt Rivers and remained open until the mid-1960s. During its latter years I well remember as a small boy being held spellbound by the wonderful exhibits during occasional family excursions. I am sure those visits made a lasting impression on me. Eventually, in 1977, the remaining exhibits were transferred to Salisbury Museum where an excellent Pitt Rivers gallery describing his work has been created. The Larmer Grounds have recently re-opened (see Places to Visit) and, although a shadow of their former glory, are once again hosting a range of musical and other cultural events bringing crowds once more to the area, which I am sure would have pleased the General.

However, the greatest legacy left by Pitt Rivers — his printed work and the bulk of the Cranborne Chase material — has been, and continues to be, a rich source for archaeologists both now and in the future.

3 Soils, pollen and lots of snails

Dr Michael J. Allen

As a professional archaeologist with strong research interests in understanding the changing environment on the chalklands of southern England, I had been aware of the research in Cranborne Chase through the General's volumes, and the work on Down Farm through the archaeological publication of *Landscape Monuments and Society*. It is an area known well to my wife, Julie Gardiner, who worked with Martin, Richard Bradley and John Barrett as a part of her postgraduate research. Until 1994, however, Down Farm was an area outside my own researches which had focused on Sussex, Hampshire, and Wiltshire concentrating on Stonehenge, although I had also worked extensively close by in the Dorchester landscape. It wasn't until a phone call from Richard Bradley telling me about one of Martin's sites (the Fir Tree Field shaft) that I became involved. Richard thought it might be useful for me to examine the environmental potential of this feature. Little did I realise that the site visit, prompted by Richard Bradley's enquiry, would lead me, as it had many others previously, into a long-standing fascination with this area. I initially wanted to undertake some limited analysis for Martin. The opportunities offered by the amazing sites excavated by him on Down Farm could not be missed. My interest became so great that over the next five years I was to remove nearly half a metric tonne of soil from Down Farm and its environs and spend many of my weekends and evenings peering down microscopes, identifying, counting and recording over 125,000 broken and microscopic snails from this area. Why? Because this provided the opportunity to start to understand what the landscape looked like as prehistoric peoples knew it. It allowed us to begin to understand why people were here, what they were doing, what resources were available, and ultimately how they changed, altered and modified their original landscape out of all recognition and largely created the beautiful downscape we see today. Detailed below are my preliminary thoughts and understanding of this changing landscape. There is more detailed mapping yet to do.

Unravelling landscape, environment and land use

In order to understand how past communities existed and lived among the monuments they built and the debris they left, it is important to understand the landscape which they inhabited. The downland landscape, vegetation and farming patterns are largely a product of the twentieth century, albeit much of which has its inheritance and origin in our ancestors six millennia ago. The landscape we see today is not one that would be recognised by the hunters and first farmers; only the general shape and form remains — the rivers, climate, vegetation, wild animals and pattern of land use have all been transformed.

The wider landscape provides the basic stage upon which communities lived and their activities were constrained. It provides the resource base and potential in terms of the flora and fauna, ie. food, fuel and shelter. Examining the evidence of past landscape and of landscape change can help us understand the development of how prehistoric families used and lived the landscape in terms of clearance, farming and cultivation, and how the consequences of any changes were met by those communities. In effect the landscape is as important as the sites within it; it is more that just the backdrop to the stage, it is integral to, and defines the parameters of human activity (environmental possibilism).

There are three distinct elements which contribute to this understanding and aid in interpreting landscape change in our study area. First are climatic changes that have occurred over the past 10,000 years and have been well been documented (summarised in Table 2). This table shows changes in the vegetation as a consequence of climatic development — but these changes are listed only at very general scale. The changes that occurred at Down Farm, also occurred in Manchester, for instance.

To focus on southern England, we can draw on research conducted over the past 50 years, and particularly that of John Evans since the 1970s. He has provided a general scheme of development and human modification of the southern chalkland landscape (see Table 3). When I started work on Down Farm I was, therefore, equipped with this broad and generalised understanding of the evolution of the chalkland landscape. It deals, however, with the whole of southern England as a uniform mass and, as such, only provides us with a generalised outlook of anywhere on the chalklands of southern England. What Martin and I wanted to do was to go back in time and 'see' the landscape at Down Farm as the Mesolithic hunters or the Bronze Age farmers had. Could we put ourselves in their shoes (see Allen 1998)? What did the landscape look like viewed from any of the monuments during their use? This is a tall order. We are attempting to ask questions rarely addressed at this level by archaeological science. It is easy to look at the tables above and provide a general scheme, but to provide a map of land use over any specific area requires significantly higher resolution of data than employed almost anywhere else in British archaeology. Only large research projects in Dorchester in the late 1980s (and published in 1997) and at Stonehenge in the mid-1990s have really attempted this.

How do we do this? There are a number of ways we can record the past changing landscape: the preserved animal bones indicate what animals were hunted and farmed; identifying charcoals reveals the wood used and trees that grew; microscopic pollen could tell us about the plants and trees that grew but does not survive well in chalky soils; buried soils provide insights to the vegetation and of activities such as ploughing; but the most universally preserved 'microfossils' are snail shells. There are over 100 species of 'snail' and they tend to prefer different food, shade, moisture or habitat conditions. Although no single species or individual snail can tell us all about a past habitat on its own, a whole group of snail shells collected from a dated archaeological soil sample can. Normally we only see two or three of the larger snail species, often on our garden plants! All of the 'useful' snails are smaller than the garden snails, many are microscopic, their shells being only a couple of millimetres when fully grown. They are recovered through sieving and detailed time-consuming work under a microscope. Each bag of soil analysed (normally 1.5kg) may contain up to 3000 shells; most contain a couple of hundred.

What Down Farm has, that most other chalkland landscapes lack, is a 'Martin Green' and a concentration of good sites. Put these two together and you get a series of well-dated, well-excavated sites within a very small area. With analysis from a number of sites

Climatic zone	Pollen zone Godwin/West	Archaeological period	Climate & vegetation	approx. date cal. BC/ (uncal. bc)
FLANDRIAN				
			Deterioration	
Sub-atlantic	VIII	Roman period Iron Age Late Bronze Age	Cold and wet, general deterioration. High rainfall. Decline of lime. Increase of ash, birch and beech	
----------------------- Fl. III -- 1100BC				
			Stable	(950bc)
Sub-boreal	VIIb	Middle Bronze Age Early Bronze Age Final Neolithic	Warm and dry, low rainfall, wind-blown deposits. Woodland regeneration in southern England	
--- 2500BC				(2000bc)
		Late Neolithic Middle Neolithic Early Neolithic	Declining warmth. Landnam and first agriculture. Elm decline:- 3350BC/(2300bc)	
--- 4000BC				(3200bc)
			Optimum	
Atlantic	Fl. II VIIa	Later Mesolithic	Climatic optimum, warm and wet. Increase of 2°C, poly-climax forest. Increase of alder, some clearances	
--- 6000BC				(5500bc)
	VI		*Ameliorating* Continental climate, warm and dry.	
Boreal		Mesolithic	Assynchronous expansions of mixed oak	
	V		forest with hazel and successional from pine	
----------------------- Fl. I --- (7500bc)				
			Rapid Amelioration	
Pre-boreal	IV	Early Mesolithic	Sharp increase in warmth at 3800bc. Birch, juniper + pine woodland	
--- (8300bc)				
LATE GLACIAL				
Loch Lomond/ Younger Dryas Stadial	III	Later Upper Palaeolithic	Sub-arctic climate; Loch Lomond readvance Tundra	
--- (9000bc)				
Windermere (Allerød) Interstadial	II	Later Upper Palaeolithic	Interstadial, rapid amelioration. Birch, pine, and tundra	
--- (11,000bc)				
Late Devensian	I	Later Upper Palaeolithic	Sub-arctic climate	
--- (c. 14,000bc)				
Main Devensian		Upper Palaeolithic	Sub-arctic climate, full glacial advance Man absent from British Isles	
--- (c. 22,000bc)				
MID GLACIAL sub-arctic - Upton Warren - Interstadial		Earlier Upper Palaeolithic ? Mousterian	Sub-arctic climate -, interstadial	
sub-arctic -			Sub-arctic climate	
--- (c. 60-70,000bc)				

Table 2. Table outlining climatic zonation, basic vegetational change and archaeological events for Southern England. This enables pollen zones quoted in many specialist pollen and quaternary geography reports to be equated to the archaeological chronology and activity

of differing ages in this small area we can start to build up a picture of past landscapes. Archaeologically each site may have been occupied for relatively short periods of time, but the ditches and pits often provide reservoirs of soils and sediments accumulating over several centuries, if not millennia. We hope to be able to produce maps of the land use over Down Farm from the Mesolithic to Iron Age rather like I have done previously for the Stonehenge area (Allen 1997). But the information here is much better. At the time of writing these maps are still under construction but will follow, and from them will come a more detailed understanding of the prehistoric use of Down Farm over six millennia. Until that is done I wish first to describe some of the basic changes in the landscape from the Mesolithic to Neolithic periods and then, in the later Neolithic, guide you on a walk down the Allen Valley.

LANDSCAPE, ENVIRONMENT AND LAND USE IN CRANBORNE CHASE

For the earlier archaeological periods there is relatively little information and we are forced to take our interpretations from more country- , or at best region- , wide generalisations. Very rare snapshots of time are, however, preserved in peats buried within the Allen Valley. Pollen from these of late glacial date, probably about 12-13,000 years ago, indicate an episode when open, species-rich grassland existed with plants typical of todays Arctic and Alpine areas, and the River Allen was larger and deeper. This evidence is very rare indeed for the chalklands where pollen is not usually preserved. Only one other site in the country, at Folkestone, has a similar record.

Mesolithic

I start my narrative in the Mesolithic, when we have some information from Down Farm of the local landscape in which the Mesolithic hunters walked. Most of this evidence came from one feature: the Down Farm shaft. This natural feature is so unusual and has provided such important environmental information that the description of the feature, its archaeological content, and environmental interpretation, are warranted. The following Mesolithic text may seem unduly long, but it covers a period of six thousand years in which we have evidence of widespread activity and nationally important environmental data. There is one other clue, however, to the earlier Mesolithic environment, from the Neolithic Cursus.

The Cursus

The first Mesolithic environmental evidence we have is difficult to explain, because it comes from the ditch of the Neolithic Cursus in Chalk Pit Field. A detailed programme of snail analysis by Roy Entwistle and Mark Bowden included a series of nine samples from this Cursus ditch. The lower samples produced evidence of deciduous woodland with some local small openings. This was assumed to indicate the earlier Neolithic woodland. However, it differs from the evidence from the base of the Cursus ditch 600m to the south which indicates a grassland landscape around the Cursus in Fir Tree Field. By examining

Period	Environment
Medieval/Romano-British/Iron Age	Intermittent cultivation and grassland. Formation of ploughwash deposits
Bronze Age	Open environment of grassland or arable. Cultivation/grazing intermittent. Formation of wind-lain material
Late Neolithic	Woodland regeneration. Not at Woodhenge
Late Neolithic	Construction of henge monuments
Neolithic	Woodland clearance. Ploughing and possibly other forms of tillage. Ploughmarks at Avebury
(Mesolithic) Atlantic (?)	Dense woodland. Recorded only at Avebury, but probably at most sites
Mesolithic Boreal (?)	Open woodland. Evidence of fire and possible influence of Mesolithic man (Evans 1972, 219, 256)
(Upper Palaeolithic) Late-Glacial	Subarctic environment, probably tundra. Formation of periglacial structures and wind-lain material

Table 3. Main environmental events on the chalk of Wiltshire and Dorset in the late-glacial and post-glacial periods, from Evans and Jones (1979, 209) also re-worked and republished by Entwistle and Bowden (1991, table 2)

Roy and Mark's data in the light of my new research, together with anomalous Mesolithic radiocarbon dates, we can now offer an alternative interpretation. Chalk Pit Field has produced diagnostic Mesolithic flints but they are thoroughly mixed with the extensive later Neolithic found there. The two radiocarbon dates obtained from bones in the Cursus ditch within this scatter gave dates of 5640-5140 cal BC and 5980-5560 cal BC. These bones were clearly residual and relate to a former Mesolithic occupation. It seems likely too that the snails are also residual; all of these 'finds' being derived from the Mesolithic soil through which the Cursus ditch was dug, and which eroded into the ditch. What Roy and Mark may have produced is a rare and early glimpse of the Mesolithic environment in the chalklands of Dorset. It suggests deciduous woodland with some small clearings or openings where hunting, culling and flint loss occurred. It would seem that this Mesolithic activity was local and transitory. It is at this point that we can return to the shaft.

The Down Farm shaft

This remarkable feature revealed an exceptionally rare, unbroken sequence of deposits dating from at least the later Mesolithic to the early Bronze Age. It was discovered by Martin as a clear circular crop mark nearly 10m in diameter **(21)**, betrayed by the much greater luxuriant growth of the grass at this spot. No previous indication of its existence had been suspected despite intensive fieldwalking and aerial observation, and the fact that it lay within a five-minute walk from Martin's house!

Martin started to excavate this crop mark in 1992, first encountering a layer containing exclusively Beaker period pottery and flintwork. Below this was a sequence of layers containing mid - late Neolithic pottery of the Peterborough tradition followed by layers producing a few sherds of earlier Neolithic plain bowl. The lower layers of the 3m deep weathering cone (L7 & L7a) produced no pottery but bones exclusively of wild animals (aurochs, deer and pig) and flintwork — the only diagnostic pieces of which were all Mesolithic (Green & Allen 1997). This included a group of seven microliths found in fresh condition and in very close association. Five were of 'rod' form, a type which is uncommon in the area. It seems quite likely that these were hafted as a composite tool or weapon when they came to rest in the shaft. A radiocarbon date from an aurochs bone at this level indicates a dates of 4340 - 3990 cal BC. This falls within the late Mesolithic - early Neolithic transition, a time when rod microliths commonly occur. However, no conclusive contemporary Mesolithic site has yet been found in the area. The excavations to this stage revealed stratified layers within a very large weathering cone, beneath which lay a deep shaft infilled with almost artefact-free chalk rubble interspersed with dark, organic-rich lenses. The shaft itself was 4 - 5m in diameter with irregular, but essentially vertical, eroded sides. In the summer of 1994, the water table was reached at a depth of 13.2m and excavations were abandoned. Further excavation seemed impossible and fruitless, and augering showed that even at 25.2m (83ft) below the surface the bottom had still not been convincingly reached.

The upper 7m of the primary shaft filling consisted of chalk rubble interspersed with ten main dark organic-rich soil lenses which contained no diagnostic artefacts. The skeletons of two young roe deer were uncovered within the chalk rubble that had accumulated from the weathering and eroding sides of the shaft. They had probably fallen in accidentally, died, and their bodies been covered by the gradual natural infilling. Two seams of poor nodular flint outcropped in the side of the shaft at 3.5 and 5m. Some loose nodules from these seams had been tested for knapping suitability, but this appears to have been an incidental activity taking place when the shaft was already substantially filled. Below the lowest black soily lens at nearly 10m from the surface, a further 3m of degraded chalk rubble bands, devoid of artefacts, were encountered before a layer of much larger chalk blocks was reached and this is where excavation was abandoned. Augering showed the soft waterlogged chalk continuing for another 12m.

A series of 17 radiocarbon dates from the upper 7m of the fill of the shaft and the weathering cone provides the date and rate of accumulation of the sequence (Allen & Green 1998). The chalk rubble fills, including the two young roe deer, all centred on the late fifth millennium BC. They prove that over 4m of coarse rubble accumulated very quickly — at the most over a few hundred years. The lower fills of the weathering cone which included the Mesolithic microliths, accumulated at the same rate and over the same period of time (about 4300 - 4150 cal BC).

The rate of accumulation given by the radiocarbon dates is very fast and clearly shows the date of the fills of the excavated portion of the feature dates to the late Mesolithic. But how was it formed? A human agency is most unlikely and there is no evidence of either human production of the shaft, nor of any debris discarded during its excavation. We can only conclude that it must a have natural origin. Solution hollows and dolines are widespread on the chalk. In Dorset most originate by water percolating though overlying acid clays and soils, dissolving the chalk and enlarging already weak fissures. Elsewhere in Dorset, even where these clays have been eroded away, substantial residues and clay-rich deposits are found in these features. No trace of any such clay or residue was found within, or close to our shaft. However, the shaft does lie within a few metres of deeper

21 This splendid crop mark appeared in 1990 and revealed the site of the Fir Tree Field shaft

Coombe Deposits, in which lie the naleds discussed in the introduction. The naleds were created towards the end of the Ice Age and it is possible that the water unleashed by thawing ice may have percolated deep into the chalk and eroded fissures and channels producing 'cave systems'. Subsequent partial collapse of these systems could account for local subsidence and the creation of features such as the shaft. Although its origin still remains open to speculation, the feature has provided a long, dated and unprecedented environmental sequence spanning not only the Mesolithic/Neolithic transition but also the Neolithic/Bronze Age one as well: a sequence unique for the chalklands of western Europe.

So what has this information told us? The dark humic lenses in the shaft **(22-23)** were comprised of soil, leaf litter and other organic debris that accumulated on temporary surfaces during the shaft infill. The environment around the shaft during the later Mesolithic (dated here to the early fifth millennium BC) seems to have been a closed but light forest providing ideal cover for deer, but also for the flowering and fruiting of hazel trees. Some red deer bone between the soil layers was butchered (*see* **15**) indicating Mesolithic hunting within the open forest. This is in a period when we should see good woodland of the 'climatic optimum' (Table 2 and 3), which we have inferred existed in the slightly earlier evidence (mid-sixth millennium BC) washed into the Cursus ditch. The difference seen here indicates a slightly different picture of local vegetation, possibly created by the presence of the 'great shaft' itself. In a short space of time, although the rate of infill remains constant, a change is revealed in the local landscape. The once open woodland became denser with deciduous trees forming a good leaf litter layer, more typical of our regional and national conception of the later Mesolithic landscape (primeval forest). Perhaps the most significant evidence is of the creation of a progressively larger clearance within the wood which followed and occurred at the same time as the hafted microlith weapon was lost; perhaps hurled into the almost infilled shaft in pursuit of red deer or aurochs, the isolated bones of which were found here. This clearance is radiocarbon dated about 4350-4000 cal BC and is one of the first recorded woodland clearances in southern England. Here it might have been created to attract wild animals to graze and browse on the lighter vegetation, and provide an ideal hunting ground. The depression left by the 'great shaft' may have given ritual significance to the area, as well as providing a convenient culling basin. After a time woodland re-colonised the clearing, re-enforcing our indication of the transient nature of Mesolithic activity in the area. Although the environmental evidence from the shaft continues into the Neolithic and Early Bronze Age, it is better to deal with these chronologically with our other evidence.

Earlier Neolithic: the first farmers

Evidence of the primeval deciduous forest is widespread in southern England and can be seen from the buried soils under long and bank barrows, and from causewayed enclosures at Hambledon Hill, White Sheet Hill and Maiden Castle. Local clearance of woodland can be seen at the time of the construction of, and for access to these monuments. But evidence from the Down Farm area specifically is less obvious.

At Hambledon Hill the causewayed enclosure built in 3660-3380 cal BC was hewn out of ancient woodland, so it existed as a bare hilltop island looking over the wooded vales around. Some other areas, apart from the hilltop, may also have been cleared for pasture for cattle, plots for cereals and for access to and fro across the land. At White Sheet Hill, another hilltop site slightly further afield was enclosed by extraordinarily deep discontinuous ditches cut nearly 4m into the chalk. This site is slightly earlier than Hambledon and is dated to 3780-3370 cal BC. My own research here, from the land snails, indicates that this hilltop site was also fashioned from the primeval woodland allowing its visitors to see over the trees into the surrounding landscape from the cleared hilltop. Although cattle, sheep and pigs were herded, husbanded and corralled at both of these sites, emmer wheat was also grown. This is the beginning of farming, but was the grain for man or his animals? There are no causewayed enclosures in the Cranborne landscape, but the people at Hambledon on its edge, knew of its existence. The vistas from Hambledon allowed you to look towards, but not quite into, the riches of the Cranborne landscape.

Other glimpses of the Neolithic landscape can be gathered from soils sealed under large burial mounds or long barrows, and those which eroded into their flanking ditches. There are a number of such Neolithic long barrows in Cranborne, few of which have been excavated. The General's excavation and recording of early Neolithic Wor Barrow was innovative, but one of the few criticisms we can level at him today is that he took no environmental samples for snail analysis. He has left us with no unexcavated ditches to re-examine. The former is an unfair critique for this analysis was not adopted by archaeologists in the form we know now until nearly a century after his excavations. Only a few excavated earlier Neolithic sequences exist in Cranborne Chase. The Handley Down mortuary enclosure (*see* **31**) is one and it replicates that found beneath Wor Barrow and is of the same date (about 3700 - 3000 cal BC). Excavations by Steve Burrow revealed a full ditch section and even a relict buried soil beneath modern ploughpan.

The most important evidence from this site came from the poor remnants of the buried soil which just survived under the modern ploughsoil. This was the base of the soil upon which the builders of the Handley Down mortuary enclosure walked. Snail shells carefully sifted from this soil contained a mixed fauna with some ancient woodland

22 An awkward job — environmental sampling taking place at the Fir Tree Field shaft in 1992

species. There was some indication for the gathering of timber from the deciduous woodland before the wood was cut down to make way for the construction of the mortuary monument. Evidence of both ancient woodland and of limited local interference was seen in samples from the base of the mortuary enclosure ditch too. Most striking is the persistence of the woodland. Despite the effort in clearing it, and in the construction of an important monument to act as the stage for ceremonies of death, the site was not maintained. The snails and analysis of species diversity indices, mathematically calculated from this data, indicate that when the woodland was cleared for the monuments, the clearing was not very large. So it is possible that you could not see over the trees into the headwaters of the Allen Valley, unlike the causewayed enclosures where trees were cleared far enough down the slopes to allow you to look out over them. What's more is that, in the few hundred years that followed the digging of the ditches, the woodland grew back around, if not over, this place of funerary activity. Can we therefore suggest from the environmental evidence that it was the creation of the monument and events associated with rituals of death that were important, and not the location of interment as we recognise in death today? The wooded nature of this hillslope persisted throughout prehistory and possibly into post-Roman times.

Unfortunately the 1933 excavation of the Thickthorn Down long barrow sited, on the prominent hilltop at the southern extremity of the Cursus, was very early for the collection of snail samples. Nevertheless, samples were collected and analysed with some sophistication by A.S. Kennard for the excavator, Col Drew (Drew & Piggott 1936). Only

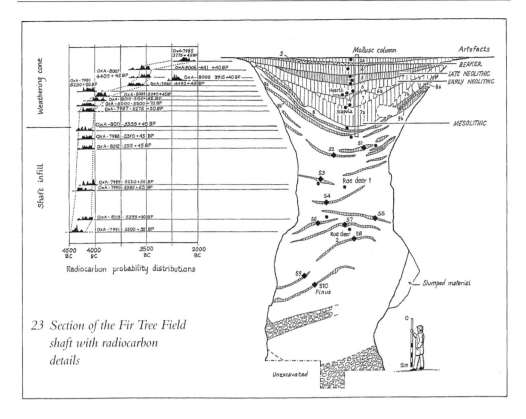

23 *Section of the Fir Tree Field
    shaft with radiocarbon
    details*

a few 'spot' samples (eight in total) were examined in comparison with long contiguous columns of 27 samples at the Handley enclosure. Nevertheless there is a hint that, although built in a woodland clearing, the woodland around the Thickthorn long barrow did not persist as long.

Like the causewayed enclosures and Handley mortuary enclosure, the Cursus too was a monument that cut a swathe through the dark Neolithic woodland. However here, unlike the causewayed camps, although woodland was felled along its entire path, not all of this had been cleared for this grand monument **(colour plate 6)**. Land snail analyses reported by Roy Entwistle and Mark Bowden (1991) indicate that some clearances may already have occurred along its path, such as in Fir Tree Field and probably at the Thickthorn terminal too. Nevertheless, their analysis indicates that the trees were cleared from the site and around its edges but that large areas of ancient woodland existed almost untouched. Although some trees would have been periodically felled, or natural glades occurred, the woodland continued to regenerate.

The final monument of this period I will deal with is the pit at Monkton Up Wimborne that Martin will discuss in more detail later. It is located in Higher Plain Field and is a perfect 'viewing platform' for the former terminal of the Cursus on Bottlebush Down, across the Allen Valley towards the Thickthorn terminal and over Gussage Down, whose long barrow is prominent on the skyline. Full advantage was taken of the topographic form of this flat hilltop. When monuments were constructed on it, the entire 'plateau' of land was cleared enabling similar views to those we have today of the Cursus and of Wyke Down. This site marks a change in landuse as well as society, it is a pre-cursor to the henges that followed, but viewed the Cursus and long barrows; central places in the landscape of the mind. A real effort was expended to clear the woodland which extended well beyond the confines of the marked 'site' at Monkton Up Wimborne. The area was maintained as short grassland by grazing herds of cattle and sheep **(colour plate 10)**. Removal of the trees was not just to clear an arena for the site, now the area of occupation and other activities were cut well into the wildwood.

In Cranborne, as at Hambledon, we can suggest that cereals were grown, not in fields but in small plots, more akin to gardens or allotments. They did not need tending the year round, so there was no need to have a permanent farm nearby. Herds of cattle were followed, sheep and pig kept. The diet included beef, mutton and hunted game, milk from cow, goat and sheep as well as a wide variety of wild fruits. Cereals were a good supplement and were a food that could be stored through the winter, but they were not the staple component of the diet. If the cereals in one or more of the garden plots failed, or were eaten by animals when unattended, it was not serious; there were plenty of other things to eat and drink.

Later Neolithic: a walk through the beginning of an organised land

The Allen Valley was a hive of activity in the later Neolithic and we have more detailed environmental information so I can guide you on a walk in space and time, down the valley, from the north-west of Down Farm to Knowlton. As we start our journey at the foot of Handley Hill, we can see some sites of previous earlier Neolithic activity. Woodland exists, but much of it is now more open secondary woodland. Some primeval forest exists and some of the woodland may still have been home to the odd family or lone bear. Elsewhere, the felling of trees and old abandoned campsites are visible. The woodland canopy is lighter allowing the sun into the woods and vegetation and brambles to grow. Animal paths are sliced through the woodland and in other places well-worn tracks and thoroughfares run across them.

A number of glades and clearings exist providing a perfect place to rest, light a fire and sharpen tools, or make a few more. From these clearings we can see onto the hilltops to the south where a belt of open grazed land in which the Cursus runs, sweeping over Gussage Down with the long barrow on the skyline. To the north, at the head of the Allen Valley, we can just see through the woods to a lighter patch with more shrubs marking another scarred site, that of the Handley mortuary site. Beyond this, and to the west, woodland extends onto the hillops (Sixpenny Handley and Rushmore) with thick clay soils, upon which a number of vantage points and clearings can be seen. The valley floor in front of us, however, is broad and wet with grass and clumps of dry reeds and rushes. The trees, in the main, start on the drier slopes, especially on the north side. As we approach the Cursus in 2950-2500 BC we come to Wyke Down, which is scarred by a concentration of activity largely on the north side of the Allen. This busy area reveals a concentration of small sacred ritual monuments and buildings belonging to a settlement. We can see from here to Down Farm itself, across an area of rough grazing with only a few shrubs and hawthorn bushes between. In Fir Tree Field can clearly been seen another centre of activity and grazed grass with a round burial barrow, pits and settlement. But beyond, the slopes of Gussage Down are largely wooded, all but the 150m wide tract through which the Cursus passes.

We are in the heart of a healthy land and of small communities: there are cattle browsing, sheep grazing and pigs in the woods. Previously small plots of land were set aside for cereals and left untended, but now such areas, although small, are tended and bounded in a fashion. The bourne in the valley flows across the grass for much of the winter, subsiding in the summer to a muddy track which we can follow. Passing Wyke Down we can see a large well-tended area on the hillslope to the north, huge timber posts mark the site of the former sacred complex at Monkton Up Wimborne. As the wind blows, plumes of dust rise from the open, recently arded plots, awaiting planting. If we revisit these later in the summer they will be wild with colour; the browning emmer, barley or oats mixed with leguminous plants, fat hen, and possibly poppies, charlock and other wild flowers, surrounded by patches of couch grass.

As the Allen Valley turns south, so we follow the broad river into a landscape of open woodlands, mixed with rough pasture, and denser woodland in patches on the slopes. Although this area is less busy, there is evidence of people all around us, perhaps not as burial mounds, sanctuaries and sacred sites, but as areas of woodland cleared for fires, timber and for grazing. Some areas have been recently used, others are now a tangled mass of brambles and hawthorn with hazel and other small trees struggling through. In front of us at 2900-2400 BC, as the floodplain of the Allen widens out, are some massive embanked sacred sites set in large open-grazed areas below the wooded slopes of Knowle Hill. Behind the first grassed enclosure (Church Henge) is a much larger more spectacular enclosed area (Southern Henge) with arable plots right up to the outer bank, and a massive gleaming chalk mound.

As we reach these sites at Knowlton we come to the end of our short 7km walk; we have noticed buildings, the taming of the landscape and the growing of cereals. I have said little of the soils, but they are thicker brown earths and brown rendzinas, perhaps up to 50cm thick. They are very silty with very little chalk in them until trees blow down or ditches and postholes are dug and chalk spread around, and they are very fertile. Cereals are growing in areas more like fields than plots and the soils are rich. The landscape is a mosaic of rich woodland, scrub, rough pasture and grazed land and small arable grounds. As we walk down the Allen Valley in the later Neolithic we see that these sites mark the beginning of a whole new era. The fact that small communities were taking root and settling on one place meant that farming could take a larger role in life, but hunting wild animals (deer and boar and wild aurochs) was still important as were the diverse crops of fruits and berries.

Earlier Bronze Age

Towards the end of the third millennium, the economic and social foundations laid down in the later Neolithic were built upon and expanded. The Beaker phase saw new lifestyles, materials, fashions, and beliefs with a growing, but more established, economy. Old sites were revisited, refurbished and revitalised (Hambledon Hill, Stonehenge, Fir Tree Field, see Early Bronze Age Chapter 6) with a new 'wealth' created by the availability of time. Larger parts of the community were free for longer periods of time to commit themselves

24 Crop marks near Pentridge reveal the site of another shaft, a small henge and an irregular feature. This latter feature produced burnt material when augered

to tasks of social and religious need rather than food procurement. Among other things, the new ideas and materialism manifest themselves in the archaeological remains, as Martin explains later, and farming became established as a larger component of the communities' economy — the evidence for this landuse can be teased out of the dry environmental remains.

Our walk down the Allen Valley now would show this new found confidence in the form of man conquering the land and all he sees. The areas of old primeval forest were diminishing rapidly, though some extensive stands of ancient woodland remained. Deer still ran through the other open woods, but fewer were at risk of being regularly stalked and hunted. Most of the animals in the Allen Valley were now tamed, domesticated or tethered.

Before all of this, however, we can identify a short episode where many of the monuments were less well tended. Longer grass, scrub and some shrubs grew on and around them. This is very marked at Knowlton Southern henge, but hints can also be seen at the Wyke Down henge and the Cursus too. Strangely, at about this time or perhaps just a little earlier (3350-2910 BC), we see grasses, shrubs and possibly small trees colonising the 1m deep depression in Fir Tree Field, that marked the shaft, immediately prior to the Beaker period. It is possible that this short-lived episode reflects a period of change between the socio-economic and political systems of the later Neolithic, and before the establishment of the Beaker period and later re-use and refurbishment of many sites.

These episodes of vegetation regeneration were, individually, rapidly curtailed. The depression shaft in Fir Tree Field was first cleared of vegetation, then the area around it was tilled and grazed. Over the following couple of hundred years the shaft infilled naturally, and when it had become just a minor, possibly muddy, hollow in the grass it was capped and infilled with chalk excavated from adjacent small pits. At both of the Wyke Down henges, episodes of longer grass growth in the ditches and over the banks are superseded by a very dry open downland, probably grazed or tilled.

Defining the exact land use as an environmental scientist now becomes more difficult as the questions become more specific. Differentiating between snail faunas of woodland, long grassland and short grassland is relatively simple. But now we need to be able to differentiate between snail colonies living on grazed short grassland, from those that live in tilled, arable land. Ecologically this can be difficult, and is made more so by the fact that the surface and micro-habitat of a modern field does not equate with that of a prehistoric one. And just as today, crop rotation and fallow seasons with pasture was probably practised, so the shells we find are likely to represent more than one of these habitats or land uses.

Despite these difficulties, many of the snail assemblages associated with Beaker features, such as the upper fills of the Wyke Down henge, with the Fir Tree Field shaft and the Beaker pits next to the shaft, all show a predominance of very short, dry grazed grassland, and probably of bare soils and episodes of tillage in the vicinity. Areas of now long-established pasture with a good grassland turf were set aside for burial and whole barrow cemeteries were established. Some turf was even cut to construct the barrows as was shown from Charly French's recent excavation of the barrows in Chalk Pit Field. The precise areas of tilled land are hard to define, but the evidence of the increased numbers of charred grain we find and a wider range of cereals (oats, barleys, and wheats), point to more fields and possibly to a more sedentary life style. For some reason, we have great difficulty, as archaeologists, in finding any houses of this period in Britain let alone Down Farm. Perhaps we don't know what we are looking for.

This expansion of the open downland, pruning of woodland and refurbishment of sites was not consistent across Down Farm. At Monkton Up Wimborne, a great pit 10m across and 1m deep whose floor had been worn smooth by passing feet in the middle Neolithic, was allowed to infill with soil, and nettles, brambles and shrubs grew. This may only have been cleared at the end of the earlier Bronze Age or beginning of the later Bronze Age.

Later Bronze Age and Iron Age

By the later Bronze Age we have to return to relying on data from a more regional perspective. There are more sites and more activity in the area, the landscape had become more uniform. The analysis of snails in determining major differences between woodland and open downland is less useful. Most of the sites of the later Bronze Age and Iron Age periods were established farms: dairy and meat herds were ranched across the 'downland'. Field systems, as opposed to fields, were established on the slopes, in part to define land and ownership and community regions, and in part to arrest the erosion and loss of soil downslope.

There is archaeological evidence of full communal farms and villages; large areas of Down Farm in particular would have been farmed open downland; common grazing land with defined field systems. The soils were brown rendzinas and essentially not much different to those we see today, apart from being a bit thicker and less stony. Careful watch was kept on the animals, and different animals were gathered into the farming villages. Foxes had to be kept at bay, the larger wild animals were now tamed and domesticated; many were kept for wool and milk, so other activities such as spinning and weaving could be seen. Fields were cleared and arded in the spring and the crop picked by hand in the autumn in a rural idyll — the precursor of the landscape we see today.

4 Marking the land:
the first farmers stake their claim

The taming of the local landscape began with the arrival of groups of these farmers about 6000 years ago. The primeval forest largely encountered had to be cleared before efficient farming could be organised. In the south the chalk downs would have been relatively lightly forested and consequently saw some of the earliest clearance. By the end of the fourth millennium BC other heavier soils had been cleared whilst woodland regression was taking place on some of the areas first cleared and abandoned due to failing fertility.

These major episodes of forest clearance required the production of large quantities of flint axeheads and it appears that the best sources of flint were exploited wherever they were encountered. On Cranborne Chase the clay with flints still yield the best quality flint in the area even after centuries of cultivation. Large spreads of knapping waste found over these areas prove they were a well-used resource, but direct evidence for quarrying into these deposits has yet to be discovered. In certain flint-bearing areas mines have been located cut deep into the chalk where the high quality seams had been exploited. The nearest group discovered close to Cranborne Chase was found upon Easton Down, Winterslow (Stone 1931) on the south eastern edge of Salisbury Plain. Here, a single radiocarbon determination of 3100 BC was obtained from an antler pick although considerable later activity was associated with Beaker pottery.

Hambledon Hill

Hambledon Hill (**25, colour plate 2**) is an outlying 'island' of chalk, some 60ha in extent, which encroaches into the Blackmoor Vale in the extreme south-west corner of Cranborne Chase. Its lofty eminence is crowned by a large number of ancient earthworks, the most striking being the Iron Age hillfort on the northern spur to be discussed in a later chapter. Two long barrows, one included within the hillfort, attest to earlier activity on this chalk outcrop. Roughly in the centre of the hill is a circular enclosure first noted and described by Heywood Sumner in 1913. His pertinent observation suggesting a much older date for this than the nearby hillfort was confirmed by excavations in 1951 and 1959 (Bonney 1961). This work undertaken by the Royal Commission on the Historical Monuments of England showed the earthwork belonged to a group of enclosures with interrupted ditches termed 'causewayed enclosures' because of the segmented nature of the ditches, as first noted at the type site of Windmill Hill near Avebury during excavations in the 1920s. These enclosures were known to date from the earlier Neolithic period and finds from the Commissions' excavations confirmed a similar date for the Hambledon enclosure. During the early 1960s conversion of the downland pasture to arable, with some preparatory earthmoving, caused considerable damage to much of the causewayed enclosure and to the southern long barrow which was completely levelled.

Because of continuing plough erosion the then Ministry of Public Buildings & Works

*25 Hambledon Hill — plan
   of the Neolithic complex
   (after Mercer)*

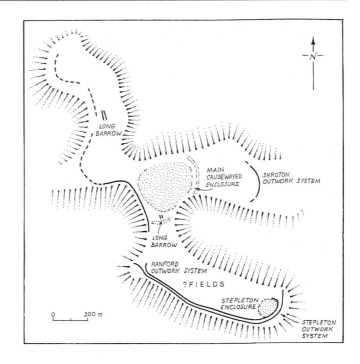

financed a major fieldwork and excavation project directed by Roger Mercer between 1974-82 (Mercer 1980). This work not only threw further light on the known areas of Neolithic activity but also revealed a hitherto unsuspected complex of earthworks practically enclosing the whole hill. The causewayed enclosure was thus only one component of a much larger site but it appears that this and the Stepleton enclosure (to be discussed later) were constructed first. About 20% of the interior of the 8ha enclosure was excavated together with a similar amount of ditch. Within the primary filling of the ditch large quantities of disarticulated human bones were found. Of particular interest was the articulated trunk of a young man consisting of the pelvis, femurs and lower vertebrae. This partially decomposed and fragmentary corpse appears to have been dragged into the ditch, possibly by animals, and was later deliberately covered by a spread of flint nodules.

Furthermore, a deliberate organic-rich deposit containing pottery, flintwork, animal and human bone was placed at intervals in some segments of the bottom of the ditch, possibly within bags, together with a number of carefully placed human skulls **(26)**. It appears that large amounts of human bone were lying about within the enclosure, which accounts for so much of it being incorporated in the ditch both by accident and design. Additionally a child burial was found placed in a niche on the ditch floor accompanied by tubular bone beads or hair ornaments, and is likely to represent a foundation deposit. After these initial phases of activity a little time elapses in which there is a partial collapse of the bank back into the ditch. Later, when the ditch is substantially filled, a series of pits are dug within the fill and further deposits of ashy material, pottery, flint artefacts and human remains are incorporated. Another short phase of inactivity allows the ditch to silt again before it is once more cut with a series of pits and slots, which are filled with the

26 Hambledon Hill main causewayed enclosure ditch section (courtesy Roger Mercer)

now familiar range of material. These features themselves are recut on a number of occasions before finally being sealed by a mounded fill incorporating much natural flint. This sequence of events reveals phases of intense activity apparently representing an almost continuous process of renewal and rededication.

Surviving pits within the enclosure sometimes contained deliberate deposits of selected material, in particular red deer antler. Other pits contained fine objects made of exotic imported materials, including stone axes of Cornish origin and pottery made of clay originating in south-west England. Two axeheads found on the surface, probably derived from pits, were made of highly prized jadeite and nephrite imported from Brittany or perhaps further afield. Further axeheads of Cumbrian and South Welsh origin were found incorporated in the filling of the causewayed ditch.

The primary purpose of this enclosure seems to have been to demarcate a sacred area within which bodies were left to naturally decompose, a process known as excarnation. Offerings to accompany the dead and appease the gods were buried nearby **(27)** and some of the defleshed skulls were placed at regular intervals on the ditch floor, perhaps to act as a gruesome deterrent to would-be trespassers **(26)**. Calculations based on the excavated sample suggest that the partial remains of some 150 individuals may be present within the enclosure ditch alone. As Roger Mercer has so dramatically described, we have to think of the place as 'a vast, reeking open cemetery, its silence broken only by the din of crows and ravens'.

A second much smaller 1ha enclosure was uncovered on the southern side of the hill

27 Hambledon Hill — reconstruction of the mortuary practices (D. Bennett)

but the evidence revealed there suggested a different function. Postholes were found, showing that buildings had probably once existed, but too few had survived the extensive ploughing to reveal their form. Pits were also found but contained a much more mundane range of artefacts, and human bone was scarcer in the causewayed ditch. The evidence suggests that this much smaller enclosure had a different function, perhaps associated with a relatively specialised group of people. These people may have been in charge of the elaborate rituals which must have taken place within the larger enclosure and at the two long barrows known on the hill. When excavated, the filling of the ditches of the smaller long barrow revealed a similar sequence to that uncovered in the main enclosure ditch, showing that the two sites are inextricably linked. The larger mound has not been excavated and lies at the protected north end of the hill.

Once the two enclosures are complete the whole chalk outcrop is turned into a fortress by the progressive construction of massive earthwork defences consisting of timber framed ramparts and causewayed ditches on all the vulnerable approaches to the hill. The southern end alone consisted of a series of three parallel banks and ditches, each about 1200m long **(28)**. The western side too had a similar length of ditch and rampart that became obscured by the much later Iron Age fortifications on this part of the hill, at the northern end of which may lie a third enclosure. Mercer has estimated that over 10,000 oak trees with the diameter of telegraph poles would have been needed to construct the timber framework of the ramparts. Analysis of the animal bones recovered from the excavations revealed a high percentage of cattle, many of which were quite elderly when slaughtered, suggesting they were mainly kept for milk production. This massively defended hilltop dominated the rich grazing land of the Blackmoor vale — which is still a major dairy producer today — and controlled the river Stour corridor to the chalk downs and coastal plain to the east. That this jealously guarded area was coveted by others is shown by the dramatic evidence of the deliberate firing of part of the fortifications. Over 200m of rampart on the south-eastern side had collapsed into the ditch as a result of the storming. Even more dramatic was the discovery of two skeletons

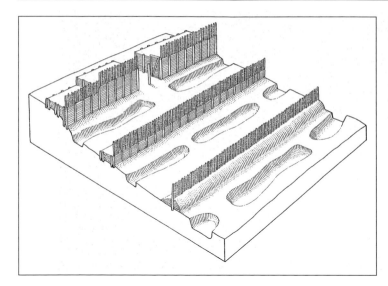

28 Hambledon Hill — reconstruction of the three ramparts which flanked the southern part of the hill. The inner rampart was of 'box' frame construction which was built of 10,000 oak beams with the diameter of telephone poles! (after Mercer)

probably linked to the attack. One, a young man, had been buried with burnt chalk probably derived from the fired rampart, whilst an older man had been buried on the floor of the ditch at the same time. Another dramatic burial found in the ditch but post-dating the destruction phase consisted of a young robust man who was found to have a fine leaf-shaped arrowhead lodged in his chest cavity **(29)**.

The apparently successful attack on the hill saw an end to any further major developments until the building of the hillfort some two thousand years later.

Burial Monuments

As we have seen, the great complex of Neolithic earthworks on Hambledon Hill also included two long barrows within its boundaries. Their original appearance must have been exceptionally striking. Cresting the hill their gleaming white form would have provided a clear statement to those who viewed them of the resident community's rights to the land. Inside the barrows, usually at the higher end, the bones of the ancestors were deposited, proof of the group's legitimate inheritance. Occasionally covering chambers or remains of wooden mortuary structures, they would also have been regarded as formal points of entry to the underworld where the gods were contacted and appeased.

About two dozen of these elongated mounds are known on Cranborne Chase - three of which have been thoroughly excavated. We know from excavations elsewhere in Britain that through their period of construction long barrows show a tendency to get smaller through time and to contain fewer buried individuals. The earlier mounds, however, generally contain what appears to be a balanced cross-section of the community, with men and women in equal numbers and with a high proportion of children, as would be expected in a subsistence farming economy. The earlier mounds also contain disarticulated bones, suggesting excarnation elsewhere. In contrast the later mounds often had complete articulated skeletons and these were mainly male. Amongst other things, this would suggest a gradual change from an egalitarian society at the beginning to a more stratified society towards the end of the period. A long barrow of this later type, known as

29 Burial found near the eastern entrance to the Stepleton enclosure at Hambledon Hill. A robust young man, he appeared to have been killed by an arrow tipped with a fine leaf shaped arrowhead which was found in his thoracic cavity. (Courtesy Roger Mercer)

Wor Barrow, was excavated by General Pitt Rivers on Handley Down (*see* **18**).

In this case the mound was 46m long and overlay a rectangular foundation trench probably for either a first phase timber revetted mound or mortuary enclosure. Parts of a small ditch associated with this structure had survived later enlargement and were recorded by Pitt Rivers, although he failed to recognise their true significance. Occasionally such structures are found without any ditch and it seems the larger ones may represent fenced mortuary enclosures where bodies were excarnated and, in the case of the smaller ones, mortuary houses where the bones were stored, perhaps prior to burial elsewhere. A number of enclosures of this type are known in the area **(30),** including one close to Wor Barrow on Handley Hill **(31)**. The latter has recently undergone a small excavation that revealed a substantial ditch over 2m deep, from which a sherd of plain bowl pottery was recovered suggesting a date in the earlier Neolithic. A further larger enclosure lies at the north-east end of the Cursus and will be described later.

Returning to Wor Barrow, the primary deposits were found as a compact mass towards the entrance to the earlier mound. They consisted of three articulated male skeletons and the disarticulated remains of three other males. It is clear that this structure was then buried beneath a much larger mound requiring the digging of a causewayed ditch 3m deep. Shortly after the building of the mound a man and a boy were buried in the ditch terminal at the south-east end. A large lozenge-shaped arrowhead found within the rib cage of the man may have been the cause of death and is reminiscent of the burial already mentioned from Hambledon.

The 'Wor Barrow complex', consisting of Wor Barrow itself and two adjacent round barrows **(32)**, chronicles a particularly interesting sequence of activity. Wor Barrow, as we

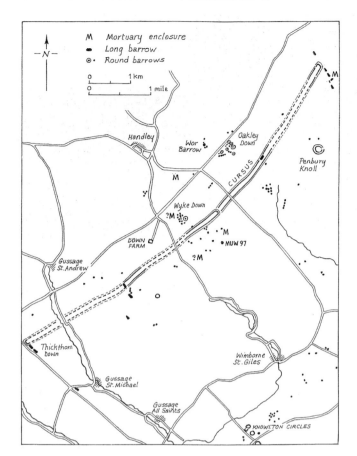

30 Distribution of monuments around the Dorset Cursus

have seen, belongs to the latter part of the long barrow building tradition when only certain selected members of society were being interred. This tradition eventually gave way to one in which single high-status individuals or double examples, sometimes furnished with grave goods, were buried under round barrows. Mounds 26 and 27 at Wor Barrow are both examples of this type of Neolithic round barrows. Pitt Rivers recorded two adult males, one buried with a jet or shale belt slider in mound 26, whilst fragments of human bone were found in the backfill of Colt Hoare's opening hole in mound 27. Both barrow ditches were irregular and appear to have been remodelled on more than one occasion. Barrow 26 possesses a causeway which points west towards the 'entrance' of Wor Barrow, and both produced sherds of Mortlake ware in their primary ditch fills, confirming their middle - later Neolithic date. Remarkably Pitt Rivers also found a crouched Beaker burial to the south-east of the long barrow. This concluded a sequence of burials which documents the changing nature of burial rites throughout the third millennium BC, and foreshadows the full floruit of round barrow construction in the succeeding Bronze age, as best seen on Oakley Down only 500m away.

The General, on concluding his excavations at Wor Barrow, used the spoil to form 'an amphitheatre with terraces, with a view to using the old surface line of the barrow as an arena for games and other amusements'. This Victorian earthwork survives today and surrounds

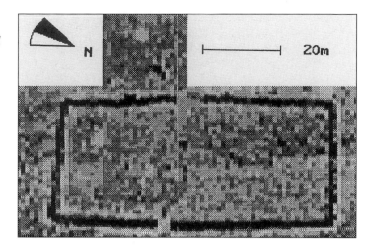

31 Handley Hill mortuary enclosure — geophysical survey (S. Burrow)

the only remaining Neolithic part of the monument — the re-excavated barrow ditch.

A number of the long barrows in the area have distinctive U-shaped or almost completely enclosing ditches, as in the case of Wor Barrow. This individual character has given rise to them being described as of 'Cranborne Chase' type. Another long barrow, exhibiting the same ditch shape, was excavated in 1933 (Drew & Piggott 1936) and can be found on Thickthorn Down which connects with the location of a further unexcavated long barrow and the south-west end of the Dorset Cursus.

Strangely this idiosynchratic long barrow covered no primary burials but recently it has been recognised as belonging to a type of mound known as a 'bayed' long barrow which often lacks burials (Bradley & Entwistle 1985). The mounds often provide evidence of a stake fence built down the long axis from which at intervals a series of shorter fences were constructed at right angles. The bays, perhaps representing division of labour, were then infilled over a period of time with rubble and earth. These vertical breaks in stratigraphy can be recognised in the photographs taken of the mound during its excavation (**33**). Why such mounds lack burials is still something of a mystery, but the absence of mortuary structures suggests that they may have been built rapidly to 'mark the land'. Perhaps the physical divisions manifest in these mounds is reflecting wider divisions taking place within society at this time.

The early radiocarbon date (see Appendix) appears to suggest it was one of the first monuments constructed in the area. However, it is now known that the antler used for the date was contaminated with preservative and is likely to be several hundred years too early. Although unexcavated, the nearby larger long barrow with parallel side ditches is likely to be earlier and lies very close to the south-western terminal of the Cursus. Sharing the same axis, this terminal bank was built on such a scale as to resemble a long barrow, thus linking the two forms of monument. Indeed, even recent writers (eg. Hawkins 1980) confuse these earthworks. About a dozen long barrows are intimately associated with the Cursus.

The Dorset Cursus

Cursus monuments have a wide geographical distribution within Britain stretching from Devon to Tayside in Scotland. They consist of two parallel lengths of ditches and banks,

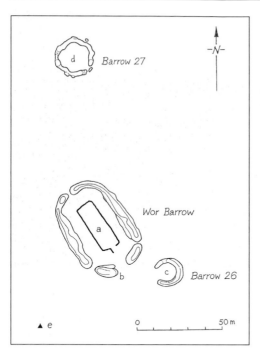

32 Wor Barrow burial complex, consisting of: bedding trench for primary timber revetted mound a. Crouched burials of a man and boy in the primary ditch fill b. Later Neolithic round barrows c and d, and Beaker flat grave e

set at some distance apart, and are closed at either end, forming very elongated rectangular enclosures. They can vary in length from a couple of hundred metres to the grandest example of all, the Dorset Cursus, which stretches for over 10km. This monument's course is rather unusual amongst its class, as it lies perpendicular to the prevailing local topography, which has a NW/SE axis. The south-west end crests the top of a ridge and during its north-easterly course crosses two further significant ridges and three river valleys. The incorporation of natural features, particularly water, seems to be integral to its design. The three incorporated streams are close to their origins and only flow for a few weeks during most winters where they are crossed by the Cursus. Aerial photography has clearly shown that the ditches cut right through two of these valleys with the course in the Gussage valley so far unresolved, which suggests a water table not dissimilar to today.

In fact, the Dorset Cursus is really two separate cursuses, both 90m wide, about 5km long, and built end to end. The earlier southern or Gussage Cursus maintains a pleasing symmetry along its course. Descending from Thickthorn Down it crosses the Gussage valley and climbs up to the next ridge, Gussage Down, where it incorporates a long barrow at approximately its half-way point. It then descends into the Allen Valley before climbing up to near the top of the next ridge where it terminates. Interestingly, close to both ends, clear evidence of earlier Mesolithic activity has been found. Underneath the excavated Thickthorn long barrow, pits were found associated with worked flints, including a microlith found in the old land surface. In Chalk Pit Field, not far from the Bottlebush terminal, an important Mesolithic flint scatter was later overlaid by another of Neolithic date. It would seem that the two locations, with a long history as important places, were linked by the monument.

Although by no means perfectly straight, major changes in the monument's alignment

33 Thickthorn Down long barrow under excavation in 1933. (Courtesy Dorset County Museum)

relate to points where it crosses the lees of hills (Bradley, 1986). At these points the proposed course would not have been visible for any great distance to those digging it, making it difficult to stay on line. This raises the possibility of simultaneous construction at different points, which were not intervisible.

The 'wanderings' are corrected by significant dog-leg stretches when a much greater length is again visible. This is particularly apparent on Gussage Hill where the incorporation of the long barrow is of paramount importance (**colour plate 4**). Crossing the Allen Valley at Down Farm a number of striking natural phenomena present themselves. The monument incorporates the Pleistocene river cliff, crosses the naleds (*see* p13, **6**) and closely skirts the shaft in Fir Tree Field, which we know was still partly open at this date. In this valley the northern ditch, as seen from the air, has the appearance of a string of sausages. The likely interpretation for this is that an earlier slighter ditch has subsequently been enlarged in sections, with not all of them being joined, leaving segments of the smaller ditch in between. However, no trace of the smaller ditch was revealed at the two points, the northern Cursus ditch was excavated on Down Farm (*see* **50**).

These excavations examined the ditch on both sides of the River Allen some 650m apart, and revealed strikingly similar ditch profiles (**34**). Trapezoidal in shape, the ditch was 3m wide at the top, 2m at the bottom and 1.4m deep. Calculations based on the construction of the entire monument by hand give a minimum figure of just under half-a-million worker-hours. Radiocarbon dating of animal bone samples found close to the base of the ditch (see appendix) has produced dates around 3300 BC, consistent with the small sample of plain bowl pottery found. A few fragments of human bone also discovered might provide a clue to its function — a point to which we will return. Above the river cliff a slight knoll is strewn with Neolithic flintwork, the largest concentration along the whole monument. Here excavations, as we shall see later, revealed major secondary activity within the earthwork. Immediately below this cliff a lake forms for a short time during most winters (**35**) and both features are neatly contained by the earthwork. From here the Cursus climbs uphill onto Bottlebush Down where it ends some 400m before

34 Dorset Cursus. Richard Bradley standing in the northern ditch, which he uncovered in Chalk Pit Field 1984

the crest of the next ridge. It was from this point, at some unknown time later, that the monument was extended for a further 4.3km, almost doubling its length and incorporating another river, the Crane. Again part of this river only appears above ground for a short time during most winters. The Pentridge Cursus covers more even terrain before ending, near further long barrows, close to Bokerley Dyke.

The long barrows associated with the Cursus are integral to its design and many throw considerable light on the sequence of construction. For instance, the Thickthorn Down terminal is at an odd angle and is not squared-off as is more usual. The reason for this seems to be that it was designed to share the same axis as the closest long barrow which we must assume was already in existence. The other nearby 'empty' long barrow, which we discussed earlier, also shares this same alignment. As we have seen, the incorporation of one of the Gussage Hill mounds involved a considerable deviation in the course of the Cursus, which can only mean that this mound was already in existence. The inclusion, in the northern bank of the Pentridge Cursus, of a long barrow near Oakley Down repeats this course of events in this later portion of the monument. The sequence at the north-east end near Martin Down appears to mirror that of the south-west Thickthorn end. Here the Cursus changes its alignment by 7 degrees, some 600m before the terminal, so that it can end next to a long barrow. This barrow is considerably lengthened by the addition of an 80m bank barrow to its higher south-east end and this in turn features an attached round barrow. The island of grass which marks the location of these monuments in a sea of arable crops today is easily mistaken as a single long barrow and not as the composite monument we know it to be **(36)**.

Aerial photography has recently revealed further monuments close to the north-eastern end of the Cursus **(37)**. These, now confirmed by geophysics, consist of a long mortuary enclosure about 100 x 25m, open at its eastern end and abutting a short long barrow at its western end. A further well-preserved long barrow lies 200m to the south, the axis of which is aligned upon the Cursus terminal. About 300m to the north of the terminal lie the ploughed remains of a further small long barrow which may have been

35 This ancient river cliff and seasonal lake were deliberately enclosed by the earthwork of the Cursus as it descended into the Allen valley

enclosed within a stone circle. During Colt Hoare's brief examination of this mound he described it as 'surrounded by sarsen stones'. Indeed, even now I have noticed large lumps of sarsen ploughed to the surface around the edges of this mound.

Putting all of this evidence together it would seem that the Cursus was built to form a grand avenue between existing groups of long barrows. Enlargement of the ends of the Cursus seems to suggest a need for the terminals to imitate the proportions of the neighbouring long barrows, thus inextricably linking the two monuments in the minds of the people. This arrangement was embellished by the addition of further mounds built either on the same alignment as the terminals or pointing at them.

The bank, probably revetted by turf or chalk blocks, and ditches of the earthwork act as a barrier. Access to the most significant points of the monument would have been restricted thus reinforcing the special status of any observers. Hard evidence for any ceremonial activity is scant but it does include the discovery of human bones within the ditch, suggesting excarnation areas may have been present, where bodies were left to naturally decompose.

The most important feature of the whole monument is, however, the alignment of the Gussage Cursus, which lines up perfectly with the movement of the sun at the mid-winter solstice. The north-eastern end of this monument terminates just below the ridge on Bottlebush Down. Observers standing here and looking back along the course of the Cursus, which would have presumably been kept free of vegetation **(colour plate 6)**, could watch the mid-winter's sun set directly behind the silhouetted long barrow on Gussage Hill **(colour plate 4).** This spectacular skyline effect would have been lost had the terminal been placed on top of the ridge. A favoured observer could watch the setting sun disappear behind the long barrow and be linked directly to the ancestors and to the Cursus itself creating a monumental avenue of the dead. The ancestors associated with this movement of the heavenly bodies would become immortal and part of nature itself. Further symbolic meaning is manifest in the position of the Cursus along the spring line where annual flooding events were partly enclosed within the monument. By linking their

36 Aerial photograph of the northeast terminal of the Cursus. In the arable field a number of other monuments can be seen — compare with figure 37 (By permission of English Heritage copyright reserved)

ancestors with the forces of nature, and the movements of the heavenly bodies through one grand structure, certain individuals were trying to gain control, or appear to have control, over life itself.

Undoubtedly restricting access to the north, the Cursus may have marked the upward limit of settlement at that period. Certainly the great concentration of contemporary settlement debris comes from the south in the Bournemouth basin area of the coastal plain. It is not until later in the Neolithic, presumably when the Cursus has fallen into disrepair, that significant expansion takes place on the high ground to the north. But even in disrepair, as we shall see, the Cursus continued to exert a magnetic influence over the way the ritual landscape was organised for a further two thousand years — an astonishingly long time when measured in human lifetimes.

Settlement Evidence

There is little evidence for settlement on Cranborne Chase during the fourth millennium BC, at least with the exception of the rather specialised complex already discussed upon Hambledon Hill. Elsewhere on the Chase only a handful of sites have so far yielded plain bowl pottery and two of these were ditches of long barrows. There is a widespread scatter of some 50 leaf arrowheads recorded across the area and only one flint scatter of earlier

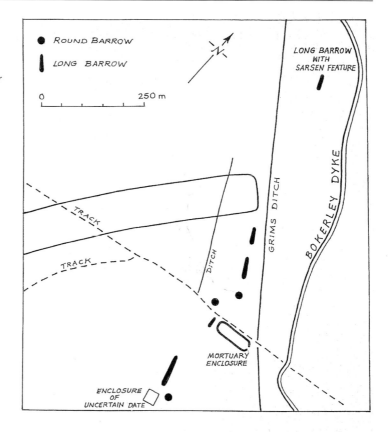

37 *The monument complex at the northeast end of the Dorset Cursus. After Bowen 1990 with additions* (By permission of English Heritage copyright reserved)

Neolithic type which partly underlay the long barrow on Thickthorn Down. It is possible that the arrowheads, not all of which are necessarily early, may once have been part of a series of discrete flint scatters which have been masked by the much larger spreads of later Neolithic material. Even allowing for this, it would seem the area was marginal to the main focus of activity taking place on the coastal plain around Bournemouth. In this latter area, numbers of pits yielding plain bowl pottery together with much greater densities of earlier Neolithic flintwork have been recorded. This distinction appears to strengthen towards the end of the millennium with the construction of the long barrows and the Cursus on Cranborne Chase. Perhaps the area was predominantly used for burial and ritual activity in contrast to the coastal plain where only one long barrow is known. Access to the clay with flints on the high ground, so favoured in Mesolithic times, would have been cut off by the Cursus and it is not until it has fallen into disrepair that settlement of this area on any scale takes place again.

The start of the third millennium BC appears to mark a reversal in the intensity of occupation between the two areas, with Cranborne Chase producing much higher densities of later Neolithic material. It is possible that over-exploitation of the previously fertile coastal plain caused this dramatic shift in settlement location, the evidence for which will be discussed in the next chapter.

5 Ritual, ceremony and consolidation:
the later Neolithic

Fieldwork has revealed major spreads of later Neolithic flintwork over the clay with flints deposits (38), sometimes covering areas in excess of 50ha (124 acres), a phenomenon increasingly noted by fieldworkers wherever this has been studied in detail (eg. Gardiner, 1984). As we have already noted in the Mesolithic, such deposits produce high-quality surface flint and occur very near to the sources of the south-easterly flowing streams, which in turn contribute to the main rivers supplying the coastal plain. In addition to these points the Neolithic people would also have been attracted by the fertile loess based soil which once covered these areas. Initial 'slash and burn' agriculture would have produced high crop yields for several generations in one place before failing fertility caused a shift to a new piece of ground. The large, almost continuous, spreads of flintwork found over these areas probably represents this pattern of land usage. However, very detailed fieldwork, as that undertaken by John Arnold on Handley Common, has revealed clusters of artefacts suggesting settlement foci within a much wider lower-density spread of artefacts (39).

Remarkably the work at Handley Common revealed a pattern of clustering, albeit on a larger scale, which shared the same locations as those favoured in the Mesolithic. This would indicate that limited clearance, already suggested for the Mesolithic, resulted in

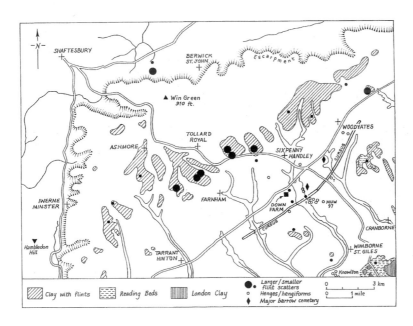

38 Distribution of later Neolithic sites in the study area

1   Down Farm in bloom — summer 1989

*2   Vertical air photograph of the chalk 'island' of Hambledon Hill. Compare with **25**.* (Dorset County Council)

3 Romano-British brooches from Woodcutts illustrated for volume I of 'Excavations in Cranborne Chase' by General Pitt Rivers. (Salisbury and South Wiltshire Museum)

4 Mid-winter solstice — Gussage Down

5 Reconstruction of the Wyke Down Neolithic buildings (Yorkshire Television)

6 *The Dorset Cursus under construction about 3300BC* (D.Bennett)

7 *Ground plan of Neolithic building 1 as revealed at Wyke Down* (Yorkshire Television)

*8   Air view of the Monkton Up Wimborne Neolithic complex — compare with **52***

9   The Neolithic 'temple' at Monkton Up Wimborne as it may have appeared about 5,300 years ago (Jane Brayne)

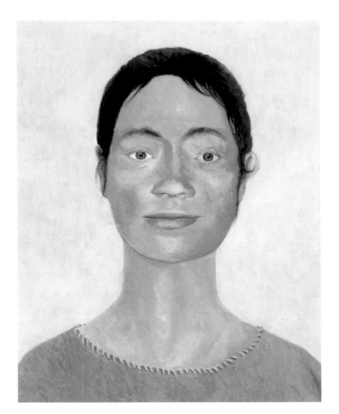

*10a Neolithic woman Monkton
Up Wimborne* (Jane Brayne)

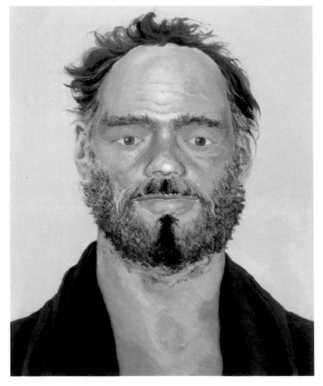

*10b Bronze Age man Monkton
Up Wimborne* (Jane Brayne)

11 Aerial view of the Knowlton Neolithic complex in summer 1995. The combination of a dry period and a crop of peas (particularly susceptible to drought) produced these spectacular crop marks

12 Reconstructed Grooved Ware vessels from Neolithic sites on Down Farm (D. Bennett)

13 The ruined church within the centre Neolithic henge at Knowlton with the Hale-Bopp comet crossing the night sky (M. Gaston/Celestial Skies)

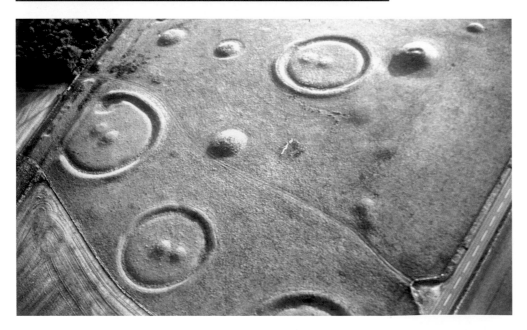

14 Aerial view of the Oakley Down Bronze Age barrow cemetery. The Ackling Dyke Roman road can be seen slicing through a disc barrow near top left

TUMULI . XXXIV . D .

WOODYATES.

15 *Early Bronze Age grave goods retrieved from the barrows on Oakley Down by Colt Hoare and Cunnington. The dagger, bone points and broken Collared Urn all came from the same burial in barrow 20 — see* **66** (Wiltshire Archaeological and Natural History Society)

16 Dr Charly French's examination of barrow 34 Wyke Down in 1998. The excavations revealed a two phased mound the earliest of which was revetted by a stake circle. Two ditches surrounded the mound

17 Cinerary Urns, and a small Food Vessel which accompanied a child burial, found during the excavations of the Down Farm pond barrow — see **70**

18 *Reconstruction of the Down Farm Middle Bronze Age settlement. By now the Cursus (top left) is over 2,000 years old and fields are being constructed right up to its edges but it was still visible and respected by those living nearby* (R. Massey-Ryan)

19 *Aerial view of the Ogden Down ceremonial complex. The timber avenue (centre) linked the two ring ditches visible at the top and bottom of the photograph*

*20 Reconstruction of the north end of the Ogden Down complex as it may have appeared about 3,000 years ago. See **84** for alternatives* (D. Bennett)

21 A bird's eye view of Hod and Hambledon Hills by Heywood Sumner (private collection)

22 Winkelbury Hill, Berwick St John. The site of some of the earliest pioneering excavations conducted by Pitt Rivers on Cranborne Chase. Outside the bottom left-hand corner of the fort a small mound and hollow can be seen. This was a supposed 'pit dwelling' uncovered by the General which he evidently did not backfill!

*23 Reconstruction at Butser Hill of the Iron Age roundhouse excavated at Pimperne. Refer to **88** for ground plan* (Copyright I.M. Blake and D.W. Harding)

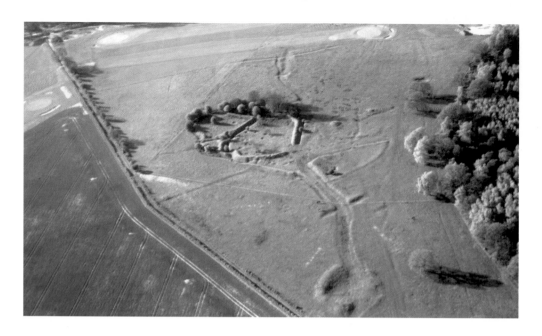

*24 Aerial view of the Woodcutts Romano-British settlement (see **95**). The apparent hengi-form enclosures near top left and top right are recently made golf-course bunkers!*

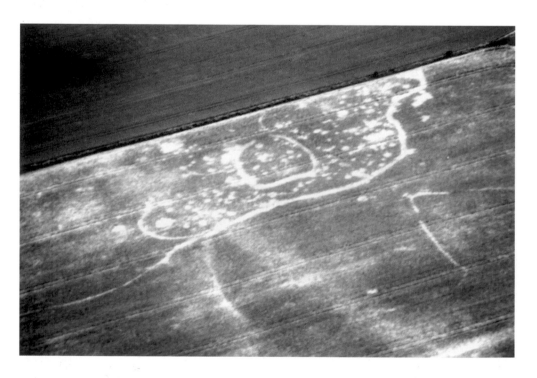

*25 A recently discovered Late Iron Age settlement on Gussage Down (see **92**). The inner 'D'-shaped earthwork probably encloses the site of a major roundhouse*

26 *Excavations in progress on the Minchington villa in 1998. Probably first noted in 1868 it was re-discovered during my own fieldwork in 1987*

27 *Gilded bronze harness mount dating to the seventh/eighth centuries AD. Although this fine piece was found on Cranborne Chase the closest parallel for it seems to be from the great Anglo-Saxon cemetery at Sutton Hoo in Suffolk. Here a male burial with a horse and complete harness was excavated in 1991* (D.Cousins)

28 The great late Roman defensive earthwork Bokerley Dyke. Probably constructed over a much earlier, Bronze Age line, even today it continues to mark a major administrative boundary — between Dorset and Hampshire. (By permission of English Heritage copyright reserved)

39 Neolithic flint scatters on Handley Common. The Mesolithic scatters are included for comparison. (after John Arnold unpublished)

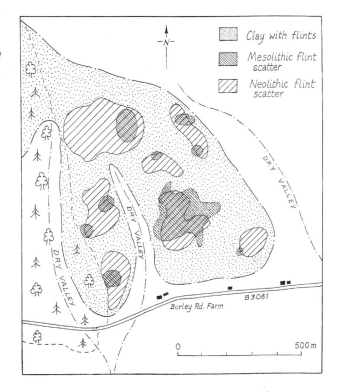

these areas bearing different and perhaps lighter vegetation, which acted as an initial focus for Neolithic groups re-occupying the same areas a few thousand years later. Amongst the artefacts recovered are a number which bear evidence of two periods of workmanship often comprising patinated Mesolithic blades or flakes exhibiting unpatinated areas of retouch produced in the Neolithic.

The flint industries themselves appear to represent good, balanced domestic type assemblages with no apparent bias towards flint exploitation. Simple flake tools (scrapers, knives and borers) comprise over 75% of the assemblages with roughly made axes and picks accounting for about 14% **(40)**. Some people have suggested that the latter were used for digging for flint close to the surface but it seems more likely they were hafted and used as tools for cultivation, similar to modern mattocks or hoes. Their even distribution over the settlement areas, not necessarily linked to flint sources, lends weight to this suggestion. Although over 8% of the assemblages comprise roughly flaked axes very few of these could be regarded as axe roughouts. Typologically most of these would normally be called Mesolithic; indeed many exhibit both true and pseudo tranchet blows **(41)**. However, patina analysis has been of great help here. Where the clay with flints is of sufficient thickness there is a striking contrast in colour between the Mesolithic and Neolithic flints found there. Indeed, so much so that there must have been a considerable time span between the two, with little evidence of continuity. Diagnostic Mesolithic flints are invariably patinated to shades of blue through to white, whereas diagnostic Neolithic forms are mostly unpatinated. The forms used in Table 4 (p67) were microliths and micro-burins for the Mesolithic, and arrowheads and polished axes for the Neolithic.

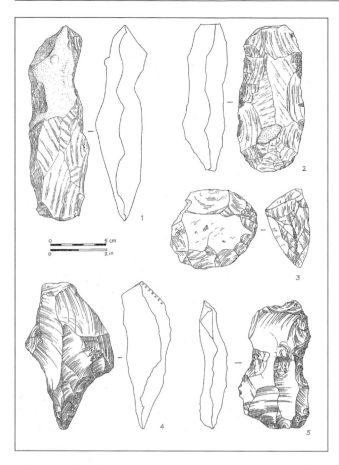

40 *Left*
Later Neolithic larger stone artefacts from the clay with flints — pick 1, roughly flaked axe in upper greensand chert 2, chopping tool 3, large borer 4, and waisted tool 5. (B. Lewis/J. Richards)

41 *Below*
Later Neolithic 'Y'-shaped and tranchet flint artefacts — 'Y'-shaped axes 1 & 2, reworked polished flint axe 3, small tranchet tool/axe 4 and tranchet sharpening flake 5. Numbers 4 & 5 were excavated from late Neolithic levels at Monkton Up Wimborne. (B.Lewis/J. Richards)

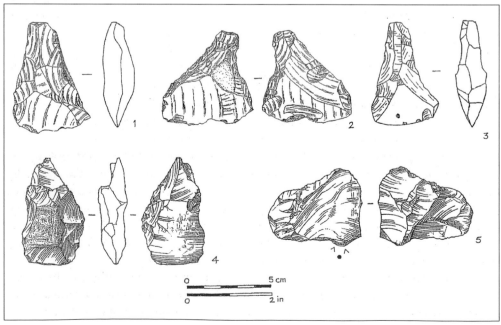

PATINA ANALYSIS TABLE

	Blue		Unpatinated		Unclassified		Total Artefacts
	No:	%	No:	%	No:	%	
Mesolithic	66	56.5	37	31.5	14	12.0	117
Post Mesolithic	4	4.6	67	77.0	16	18.4	87
Picks	8	8.8	64	70.3	19	20.9	91
Rough Axes	3	7.5	26	65.0	11	27.5	40
'Y'-Shaped Axes	1	4.3	19	82.6	3	13.1	23
Tranchet Axes	15	31.25	30	62.5	3	6.25	48

Table 4: Patination study for diagnostic Mesolithic, Post Mesolithic and undiagnostic flints from Bussey Stool, Farnham, Handley Common and Stonedown

When the same test is applied to the non-diagnostic forms such as picks and roughly flaked axes, the higher percentage of unpatinated specimens clearly shows that the vast majority belong with the Neolithic industries. The wider spatial distribution of these forms also relates far better to the Neolithic distribution than the tighter foci of the Mesolithic. The workmanship on these tools is generally simple and crude but produces a functional product. Indeed Y-shaped tools, in reality a simply made but effective form of axe, are often made on thermally fractured pieces of flint. These quite often have a natural sharp edge which can be left unmodified whilst the other end can be easily chipped to form a tapering butt to facilitate hafting. The author's own experiments have shown that this type of axe is highly efficient for splitting hazel.

Studying the polished axes provides an interesting perspective on the general crudeness of the flint technology. These, made from both flint and stone, compose only 2% of the entire tool component and 15% of the total axe numbers from these sites. They are usually found as broken fragments, many having been reworked into other forms. The axes were clearly of high quality originally but the reworking which took place after breakage was of the crude fashion characteristic of sites on clay with flints.

Indeed, several polished axe-blade fragments have been made into Y-shaped tools by the fashioning of simple tapered butts identical to the technique used on the thermally fractured pieces described above (*see* **41**). This strongly suggests that small numbers of polished flint axes were being imported alongside those produced from other rock sources. Arrowheads too were imported as shown by finds of a number in Portland Chert **(42, no. 5)**, the nearest source being the Chesil Bank some 50km (35 miles) away, strongly suggesting that some of the finer flint arrowheads may also be imports.

A number of these specific tool forms have now been found in undisputed Neolithic contexts in the area **(eg 41, 4 and 5)**. When combined with information of similar types found elsewhere in secure contexts, such as flint mines, it becomes apparent that in the

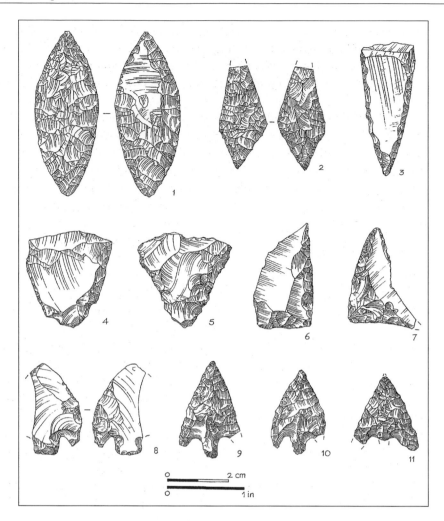

42 Neolithic and Early Bronze Age arrowheads excavated in successive deposits at Monkton Up Wimborne. Leaf 1, kite shaped 2, chisel 3-5 (5 in Portland chert), oblique 6-7, barbed and tanged 8-11 (including broken roughout 8). (J. Richards)

later Neolithic, in specific locations where there was abundant surface flint, a whole range of expedient tools were being produced by groups who were less competent at knapping flint. As the author's own experiments have shown, it was a lot easier and more economic to flake a basic axe in a few minutes into a perfectly functional form than to spend 20-50 hours on producing a perfect polished flint axe. Flaking ridges become points of weakness after prolonged use and their removal by polishing, clearly in the long term, will undoubtedly lengthen the useful life of an axe. However, if there is plenty of workable flint nearby, it is much more economic in terms of both time and effort to quickly replace an expedient tool with another.

Closer to the Cursus there is a smaller discrete cluster of sites and an outlying 'clay with flints'-type site on Pentridge Hill located on Reading Beds. This cluster close to the Cursus, particularly around Down Farm, differs to some degree from those on the main clay with flint outcrops, although with one exception they do occur on similar clay subsoil but with few of the large nodules present. It is likely that these areas also once had a rich loess capping.

The flint industries from these sites have a much lower percentage of the rough core tool element and the flake tools are generally better made. This may be due to much smaller amounts of suitable flint present in these deposits, which would account for a more careful use of the resource, but other factors could also be involved. For example there are higher percentages of 'fancy' forms including edge polished knives and a greater number and variety of stone axes. It would appear that these sites had a more specialised role to play, particularly with regard to their siting close to and sometimes actually within the Cursus itself. Parts of two of these scatters were investigated by excavation, which has thrown further light on their function and it is these to which we shall now turn.

The site within Chalk Pit Field consists of the only well-defined dense flint scatter substantially contained within the Cursus along its entire length. Crossing the Allen Valley the Cursus climbs up a steep river cliff in Chalk Pit Field which defines the western edge of the flint scatter. Above this point the soil consists of a small remnant patch of clay with flints within which the site is contained. A transect 20 x 150m across this area was selected for intensive study during the Cranborne Chase project, and was investigated through a variety of techniques, including selective excavation. The work revealed interesting spatial patterning which suggested different zones of activity (Bradley et al 1984). Some material from zone 1, next to the northern Cursus ditch, had accumulated in the secondary silts of the ditch itself and included sherds of Peterborough Ware. Bones recovered in the northern Cursus ditch produced a small assemblage, which was nevertheless rather unusual and included a high percentage of wild species as well as a few human bones. Zone 2, which covered the highest point of the site, produced high magnetic readings (suggesting intense burning), whereas zone 3 comprised the most sheltered spot in the lee of the hill and produced a high percentage of implements as well as the only pits found on the whole site. This zone appears to be the main domestic area whilst zone 4, which lay outside the eastern ditch, produced high levels of waste indicative of flint exploitation. Amongst the stone artefacts were a few (including part of a macehead and polished knives) which indicate that the site may have been of rather high or specialised status. This complex site reveals the continuing role the Cursus played in influencing the way in which activities were organised along its course. This influence spread well beyond the confines of the monument itself, as will be illustrated by the next site in our survey — Fir Tree Field.

Underlying the Middle Bronze Age (MBA) settlement at Down Farm (to be discussed later), the traces of an earlier, later-Neolithic settlement was uncovered. This consisted of a group of 16 pits and a scatter of stakeholes. The pits formed two clusters, a tight northern cluster of seven pits with an outlier and a more dispersed southern group, which probably continued beyond the excavated area. Stakeholes were confined to the area around the northern cluster and although strictly speaking undated their distribution did not seem to make sense in relation to the later MBA settlement. A few stakeholes were also found on the very edge of some pits, but none was observed to cut the filling of any of the pits. A number of the stakeholes formed arcs about 3-4m in diameter pointing strongly to the presence of domestic structures.

The southern group of pits was devoid of stakeholes and had a much greater variety of deposits within their largely homogenous fillings. An example of the special nature of the deposits can be found in pit 7 where an axehead, made of rock originating from the Graig Lwydd axe factory in North Wales, lay next to a large scraper and a boar's tusk. Pit 5 contained a remarkable banded flint pebble (43), another boar's tusk and a fragment of a greenstone axe probably originating from as far away as Cornwall. Fragmentary seashells and red deer antler were found in pit 8 whilst on the base of pit 11a, was a complete cow skull which had been placed on top of an antler pick (44a). The upper filling of this pit also contained a roe deer antler, a greenstone axe fragment and the bone of a brown bear, only the second record of the species within a Neolithic context in Britain. The deposits in the northern pits were more mundane except for two locations (24 and 32) which both contained red deer antler and an outlier (29), which had a rich assemblage with a pig jaw associated with an unbroken greenstone axe. Detailed analysis of the animal bones has produced some interesting results. The two pit clusters were analysed separately as were the outliers 29 and 11a. The results are summarised in the table below.

The results for the first three assemblages above are fairly characteristic for the later Neolithic in England, where often half of the animal bone is made up of pig. This increase in pigs at the expense of cattle has led some authors to suggest woodland regeneration, as pigs thrive particularly well under forest canopy. However, it must be remembered that most samples come from henge monuments and other putative 'ritual' sites where selective ceremonial feasting may have taken place. Indeed, at Down Farm we have seen how certain pits appear to have ritual deposits, particularly in the southern group with the exceptional pit 11a, contributing 36% of all bone found in the pits. Interestingly this pit produced other surprises: there was an unusually high percentage of cattle bones together with the only bones from wild animals (except antler) – this included a complete toad skeleton, which had apparently crawled into an eye socket of the cow skull to hibernate. Flint working debris, carbonised cereal grains and pottery (almost exclusively Grooved

	Pig	Cow	Sheep	Wild Species	Total number of Bones
Northern Pit Group	16	8	2		26
	61.5%	30.8%	7.7%		
Southern Pit Group	11	8	1		20
	55%	40%	5%		
Pit 29 only	26	18			44
	59.1%	40.9%			
Pit 11a only	5	35	4	8	52
	9.6%	67.3%	7.7%	15.3%	

Table 5: Animal bones from Neolithic pits in Fir Tree Field (excludes antler)

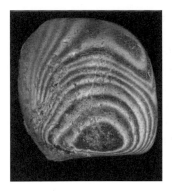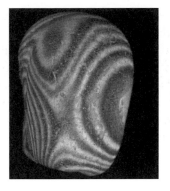

43 Three views of remarkable banded flint pebble found in a Grooved Ware associated pit in Fir Tree Field (D. Cousins)

Ware) were far more abundant in the northern pits. Radiocarbon dates were obtained from a pit in each group: Pit 11a, 4140BP and Pit 32, 4080BP.

Putting this evidence together it appears that the two groups of pits are not only separated spatially but were treated very differently in terms of their filling. The northern group with its cluster of stakeholes was most likely the remains of the main domestic area and the southern group, which is closer to the Cursus, was perhaps mainly used for ritual activity. Groups of pits such as these are likely to have been very widespread, particularly in the immediate environs of the Cursus. Indeed further stripping, only 140m to the north-east, during the excavation of the shaft, revealed three further pits of later Neolithic date. Two of these contained dark organic-rich earth with ritual deposits very similar to the pits just described. One contained a carefully placed arrangement of a remarkable nodule of flint with many natural perforations, next to an antler tine and a large cattle bone **(44b)**. When uncovered the nodule bore a striking resemblance to an animal skull and this impression was reinforced by the attendant bone and antler. It seems likely therefore that this was the deliberate intention.

A further pit contained an extraordinary broken flint axe with a splayed cutting edge **(44c)**. It is likely that this axe was symmetrical and thus double-bladed — a so far unique instance in a Neolithic context. Single-bladed axes with expanded cutting edges are occasionally found and are thought to have been influenced by early copper axes circulating at the very end of the Neolithic. This example from a Grooved Ware context is very early for such an association. Stakeholes were also uncovered at this site, many of which contributed to much repaired fence lines **(45)**. Although once again it is impossible to be sure of date, these fences stop well short of the shaft, suggesting it was still a visible feature when they were constructed. They divide up the area around the shaft, perhaps indicating sacred ground and are arranged into a series of rectangular plots, within which were pits and a few degraded postholes — probably all that remains of former buildings. Traces of Neolithic timber buildings are exceptionally rare in Britain. However, we were fortunate to find two clear examples during further excavations less than a kilometre to the north. Here, still on Down Farm, part of a remarkable 'settlement' was uncovered.

Excavations on Wyke Down have uncovered two henge monuments, to be discussed

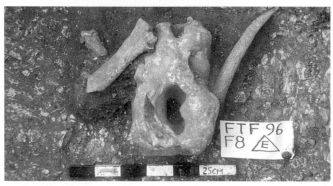

44a-d Later Neolithic ritual deposits found on Grooved Ware associated pit floors in Fir Tree Field a-c, and Wyke Down d. Cow skull and antler pick a, naturally perforated flint nodule and antler tine b, cow jaw and splayed flint axe c, dog skull and polished flint 'ball' d

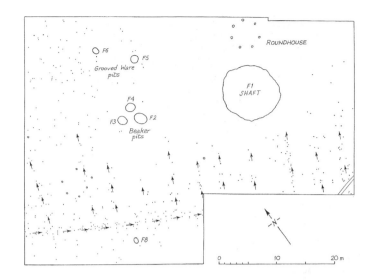

45 Fir Tree Field shaft external features including stake built fence lines

later, but of relevance here is the discovery of two Neolithic buildings associated with pits and a substantial fence line **(46)**. The site lies to the west of a second smaller henge — Wyke Down 2. Building 1 **(47, colour plates 5 and 7)** consisted of an internal 4-post rectangular setting (postholes 12-15) approximately 3.25m x 4m. Placed to the south-east of this setting was a rectangular structure about 1m x 0.7m which together with an elongated double posthole to the south-west forms an entrance to the building. To the west lay an arc of small postholes (postholes 36-40). A circle drawn from the centre point of the large rectangular element on a 4m radius incorporates the surviving arc on the west side, and this strongly suggests it was the last remaining portion of the building's outer wall. The overall diameter of 8m would also incorporate the entrance structure, which bears a similar alignment to the nearby henge. Indicated by the shallow conjoined features 16/19 are the probable remains of a hearth. Only 7m to the west lay a second building, smaller, but nearly identical in plan with a 4-post internal square element with part of an outer wall line surviving to the east. Three remaining posts survived of the entrance, which was similarly oriented to the south-east. Much charred material was recovered from the postholes of both and it is likely that they had burnt down.

This burning fortuitously preserved some much more remarkable fragile evidence — that of the fabric of the walls themselves. Substantial quantities of both clay- and chalk-based cob/daub was recovered from the postholes, together with fragments of finely smoothed plaster, bearing wattle impressions on the inside **(48)**, and with a few deep incisions on the finished outer surface. These incisions **(49)** are especially interesting because they are the remains of hand decoration that may have been cut through a painted outer surface. It is hoped that future detailed analysis may recover traces of plant or animal pigments throwing further light on the creativity of Neolithic people. This example of wall plaster, which is unique for a Neolithic context in Britain, was recovered almost entirely from the large internal postholes of the buildings, suggesting that a finely rendered and decorated enclosed wall may have defined an inner cubicle or sacred space. Comparison with broadly contemporary stone-built houses on Orkney reveals large

73

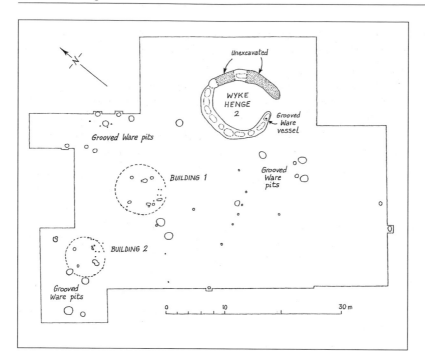

46 Wyke Down 2 henge and structures

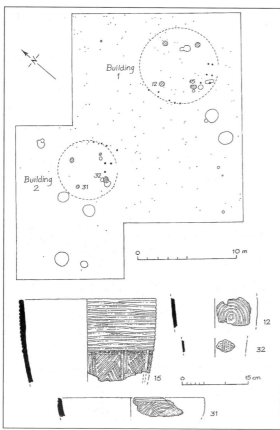

47 Wyke Down Neolithic buildings and associated Grooved Ware. Pottery numbers relate to posthole numbers on the plan

rectangular hearths or settings enclosed by the outer circular wall. Even some stone circles (eg the Stones of Stenness) enclose rectangular settings, suggesting perhaps a formal or ritualised combination of elements.

Certainly the remaining part of the outer wall of building 1 only produced one piece of daub and is likely to have been of coarser construction. In addition to the wall fragments, the inner postholes also contained substantial sherds of Grooved Ware. Their unburnt condition suggests they were placed there shortly after the building's destruction. Strikingly similar patterns of finds distribution were present in both buildings, including marine shells in postholes 15 and 32 and concentrically decorated Grooved Ware in postholes 12 and 31 (*see* **47**). This suggests a degree of formal deposition and begs the question: were these buildings part of a domestic settlement or were they perhaps temples or places of ritual activity associated with the nearby sacred henges?

Parallels for similar buildings elsewhere in Britain are few and far between but include two from Durrington some 20 miles (32km) to the north. One was discovered inside the great henge of Durrington Walls (Wainwright & Longworth 1968) and is known as the north circle and the other was found just to the south lying beneath a later round barrow (Pollard 1995). Although both are nearly twice the size of those on Wyke Down they are strikingly similar in ground plan, sharing substantial internal square settings and slighter built outer walls. Their position within and just outside one of the largest henges in Britain perhaps favours a ceremonial function.

What of the remaining features on Wyke Down and do they throw any more light on the problem? In addition to the two buildings about 20 pits, a 10m long fence line (postholes 4- 6 and 26-27) and scattered postholes were found in an area some 1500m squared to the south and west of the henge. The limits of these distributions were largely confined by the extent of the excavated area and remain to be defined by further excavation. In contrast to the pits in Fir Tree Field, most of these features were larger and contained a clear sequence of layers. However, further carefully placed deposits were also encountered here including a dog skull with a partly polished flint ball in F6 (*see* **44d**), two pig jaws in F 18 and four separate instances of a single cattle horn. Perhaps these people belonged to the Clan of the cattle horn as opposed to the Clan of the boar's tusk in Fir Tree Field!

48 Chalk based 'plaster' with wattle impressions from building 1 Wyke Down. (Wessex Archaeology)

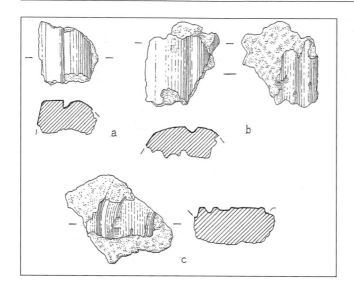

49 Externally decorated 'plaster' from building 1 Wyke Down. Fragment b (right side) depicts internal wattle impressions

Apart from these specific deposits the pits contained a range of more general material including pottery, unremarkable flintwork, animal bone and carbonised cereal grain. The evidence seems to suggest that we should not make too hard a distinction between domestic and ritual ceremonies and that ritual probably formed part of people's daily routine at this time. What we have here is probably part of an unenclosed settlement of unknown extent which includes its own religious structures.

An interesting sidelight provided by Wyke Down is that despite being carefully fieldwalked no particular concentration of flint artefacts was revealed at this spot. It is fair to say that on Cranborne Chase, as is probable in other flint-bearing areas, there is a general background 'noise' of worked flint everywhere and as a rule of thumb it seems that only much longer-lived settlement foci had higher levels of flint artefacts. It is a salutary reminder that substantial but perhaps short-lived sites like Wyke Down are unlikely to be revealed through fieldwalking in areas which produce this 'noise'.

Henge Monuments

Towards the end of the fourth millennium BC the great causewayed enclosures such as Hambledon Hill started to lose their importance and new sacred circular monuments began to appear which we know as henges. A henge consists of a ditch broken by at least one or more causeways forming entrances and which have a tendency to align on significant astronomical events such as solstices. The material from the ditch was used to construct a bank, usually on the outside to create an embanked arena. This enclosed sacred space would have been used for ceremonies, perhaps undertaken by a priestly caste, which could have been viewed by others both on the bank and in some cases just beyond. Occasionally the internal space reveals elaborate structures of wood or stone; the most remarkable example of this kind is, of course, Stonehenge. However, to date there is no evidence for such structures within the Cranborne Chase henges. During the transition period between the demise of causewayed enclosures and the start of henges a number of rare hybrid forms start to be revealed, including a new site recently excavated close to Down Farm.

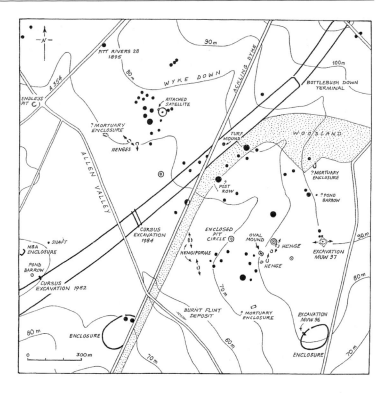

50 Neolithic and Bronze Age monument complex around Wyke Down and the Bottlebush Down terminal of the Dorset Cursus

Monkton Up Wimborne

I noticed this site on one of my periodic trawls through some aerial photographs housed at the National Monuments Record Centre in Swindon. Studying aerial photographs in libraries, or even better taking them yourself, is a wonderful way of getting to know an area. I am constantly amazed at how new sites and information continue to appear even when conditions are seemingly unhelpful for crop or soil marks. I never tire of the thrill of spotting a new site from the air, capturing it on film, and adding another small piece of information to the gigantic jigsaw.

The site in question appeared as a crop mark consisting of a clear ring of pits, some 35m across, which enclosed a massive central feature. I was most excited by this as I knew there were few, if any, parallels for such a monument. It lay in an area just south of the Cursus that through our continuing fieldwork was beginning to reveal a major new complex of Neolithic and Bronze Age monuments **(50)**. Following my visit to Swindon I persuaded Mike Allen to visit the site and auger the central feature. After much effort we eventually succeeded in augering through it to a depth of 1.5m before natural chalk was reached. Confident I was not going to be dealing with a very deep feature, I commenced excavations the following year (1997) and uncovered a site which exceeded even my high expectations.

The outer perimeter was defined by a ring of 14 unevenly spaced oval pits broken by wide entrance gaps to the east and west **(52 and colour plate 8)**. Eight were selected for excavation and revealed considerable variability in depth from 38 to 140cm and it was clear they had never held posts or stones but had been allowed to silt up naturally. Finds were

51 The Wyke Down ritual landscape looking NW (compare with 50) The excavations at Wyke Down and Monkton Up Wimborne can be seen near top left and bottom right respectively. (By permission of English Heritage copyright reserved)

few but included occasional large blocks of chalk deliberately placed at the pit bases together with, in one instance, a large cattle bone. Occasional finds within the upper fillings included a fine kite-shaped arrowhead (*see* **42, no 2**) and scraps of Peterborough pottery. Lying just outside the eastern entrance a partially surviving line of eight shallow postholes may have formed a fence that screened this entry point to the monument. Beyond the fence lay two larger postholes which could have acted as markers to those approaching the site from the east. One contained a chisel arrowhead (*see* **42, no 4**).

The interior was dominated by the huge central pit Fl (**54**), 10m wide, which had been dug 1.5m into the solid chalk to a level where a natural joint was reached in the bedrock. Digging seems to have deliberately ceased at this point, leaving a smooth natural surface at the interface between the upper rubbly chalk and the much harder blocky chalk. The surface when first revealed had an almost polished appearance as though worn smooth by the passage of feet.

When newly created it would have been a very impressive sight with its vertical sides and smooth even floor and perhaps surrounded by a low bank created from its excavated spoil. Shortly afterwards it appears to have been sanctified by a remarkable, perhaps sacrificial, multiple burial inserted into its northern edge. Thanks to specialist work sponsored by the BBC during the making of a *Meet the Ancestors* programme about the site (Richards 1999), we know a great deal about the buried individuals including an impression of the facial features of the adult **(colour plate 10a)**.

The oval grave (**53**) had been carefully dug into the wall of the great central pit partly undercutting it. Four individuals in a crouched posture had been placed within, two at either end, consisting of two girls aged about 5 and 10 years respectively, a boy of 9 years

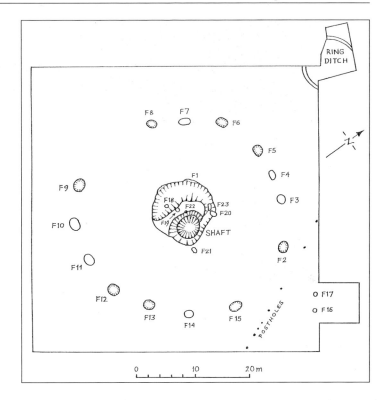

52 Monkton Up Wimborne ceremonial complex

and a woman aged about 30. Great care had been taken to conceal the grave when it was backfilled, firstly with large blocks of chalk and these had then been rammed with small shattered chalk to produce a surface practically indistinguishable from the surrounding natural bedrock.

DNA analysis carried out on the bone has shown that the youngest, a girl, was the offspring of the woman and the other girl and boy were probably brother and sister although unrelated to the mother and daughter. The youngest girl had suffered from poor health, as revealed by the discovery of a tooth abscess and a tumour on her skull, and all three showed signs of iron deficiency. None of these signs of disease were sufficient however to explain their deaths.

Isotope analysis of trace metals, which are absorbed by the body from the underlying geology through the food chain, produced remarkable results. The interpretation of these chemical 'signatures' suggested that the woman had originally lived on a high lead-level geology, the nearest match to which is found on the Mendips, some 40 miles (60km) to the north-west. She then travelled to Cranborne Chase where she stayed for some time before returning with the two older children whom she had 'acquired'. Back in the Mendips she gave birth to her daughter, the youngest child, and later still all came back to Cranborne Chase where they ended their lives. Further analyses revealed a high-protein diet most likely based on dairy products, which probably explains the almost perfect condition of the adult's teeth. The pathological evidence for iron deficiency present in the children would make it extremely unlikely that much meat was eaten. Sophisticated computer imaging was used on the woman's skull to enable an accurate reconstruction of

53 Middle Neolithic multiple grave Monkton Up Wimborne (Dave Webb)

her facial characteristics. An artist can then fill in the remaining details and we can gaze in amazement at the finished portrait of someone who lived so long ago **(colour plate 10a)**.

A radiocarbon date showed they had lived around 3300 BC, during the period when the huge Cursus was being constructed. Perhaps we have here for the first time hard evidence for the movement of people required to help construct such massive earthworks. Continued excavation in the central pit uncovered a further astonishing feature — a 7m deep shaft cut into its southern edge associated with a chalk rubble platform built around the northern edge contained within the central pit **(56 and 59)**. This platform reached the edge of the pit on the south side, giving access to the mouth of the shaft. Stratigraphic relationships showed that this had been dug shortly after the completion of the central pit, completely altering the monument. What had happened to cause such a drastic remodelling? Perhaps some catastrophe had overtaken the inhabitants and had invoked the need to dig deeper into the earth in order to placate the gods of the underworld who controlled nature itself. Certainly a series of carefully placed deposits, recalling those already seen at Fir Tree Field and Wyke Down, were made at intervals within the shaft. These included an association of a cattle skull and red deer antler beam. Nearby lay a fragment of human skull and two exceptional arrowheads of chisel and leaf type (*see* **42, nos 1 and 3)**. Additional deposits incorporated further animal bones and a number of natural although unusually shaped flints, which from their patina were clearly not found adjacent to the site.

Close to the base of the shaft lay a remarkable block of worked and decorated chalk. From its careful design it was clearly a special item, perhaps a cult object or totem **(57)**. A

54 Fl central pit Monkton Up Wimborne. The Early Bronze Age burial can be seen in the centre below the horizontal range pole. The vertical range pole is in the shaft and part of the chalk rubble platform is in the foreground

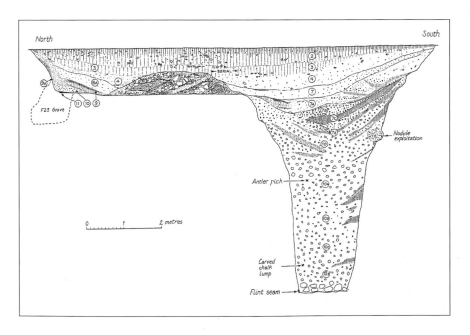

55 Section of the central pit, shaft and platform at Monkton Up Wimborne. The position of the grave F23 has been projected into the section

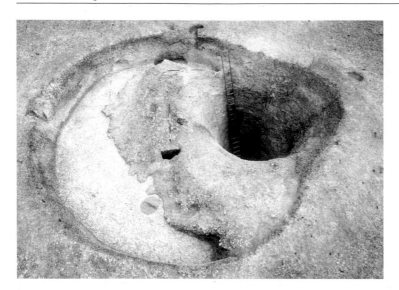

56 The central pit, shaft and platform exposed at Monkton Up Wimborne. The multiple grave can just be seen behind the top of the platform

10cm deep, carefully smoothed hole, possibly a socket, had been cut into the unworked flat side of the block with the remaining worked surfaces bearing a series of pecked lines and arcs. This type of decoration occasionally features on Neolithic stone tombs in Western Britain and Ireland and is sometimes described as 'passage grave' or 'Megalithic' art. This form of decoration may have been much more widespread on perishable materials such as the chalk plaster found at Wyke Down (*see* **48**) and wood, but as these materials rarely survive, we are unlikely ever to know for sure.

The shaft base had been dug through a thin seam of flint (**55**) which was visible in the lowest level of the wall. The final surface of the floor was thus a 'natural' unmade surface as it bore the imprint of the removed flint. Revealing such surfaces as this and then leaving them unmodified is a feature we have seen before in the F1 pit through which the shaft was cut. Exposing such natural surfaces seems to have been a deliberate act.

The shaft walls close to the base bore tool marks of two distinct forms — long diagonal grooves and areas of shallow scalloping which were left by the use of a polished flint or stone axe. The former marks were too wide to have been produced by an antler and were most likely made by a pointed stake being hammered into the wall to lever out blocks. Animal bones, mostly derived from a single piglet, lay scattered on the floor. A few of these bore clear butchery marks from a flint knife (**58**) and three larger vertebrae had been carefully tucked into the angle between the base and wall together with a worked sandstone 'ball'.

Examination of the platform within Fl showed it had been carefully constructed in at least four separate phases (**59**). Initially a 2m wide dump of coarse rubble (L16), derived from the shaft, covered much of the remaining floor area of F1. This was perhaps left for a season for a thin weathering horizon to develop (L15A). Further rubble was then piled up (L14) and both these dumps were supported by a turf revetment (L 15). This then stabilised before the predominantly earthy layer 13 was added. The latter may represent cleaning out of topsoil that had fallen into the shaft from around its southern and eastern sides. Finally a further layer of rubble (L12) was added which sealed the earthy layer 13

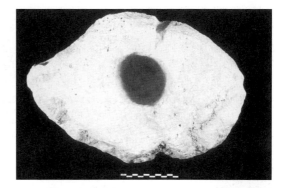

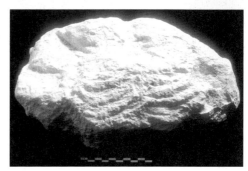

57 Three views of the remarkable decorated chalk block found close to the base of the shaft at Monkton Up Wimborne (Wessex Archaeology)

and increased the overall width to over 3m. The top of the platform maintained a width of about 1m and was highly compacted and puddled in nature. Around its northern edge large quantities of animal bone, much burnt and with a high percentage of cattle, was uncovered. It seems likely that not only did the platform provide an access point to and from the pit but it formed a focal area for ceremonial feasting and from which special offerings could be placed deep within the earth.

Earlier we saw how some of the outer pits contained large lumps of chalk that had been deliberately placed on their bases. This blocky chalk could only have come from the deeper levels exposed during the digging of the shaft; this strongly suggests the digging of the outer pits was contemporary. This would mean initially the flat-bottomed pit F1 existed alone, perhaps with a slight bank surrounding it. Then the shaft was dug and the site symbolically enclosed by the digging of the pit circle. Further rubble generated by this work could have enlarged the small bank already inferred by the digging of Fl and leaving the finished monument as it is depicted in **colour plate 9**. These different phases of activity probably took place within a short space of time, perhaps one generation, around 3300 BC.

Subsequently the earthworks started to degrade and the pits gradually filled up with chalk and earth as frost, wind and rain did their work. Fine chalky silts containing flint artefacts, including arrowheads (*see* **42, nos. 6 and 7),** accumulated in F1 during the later Neolithic, showing that the site was at least still visited if no longer used. During the earlier Bronze Age a deep soil started to develop from the annual accumulation of vegetation which was now growing rampant. Within this soil we found distinctive Early Bronze Age flint arrowheads (*see* **42, nos. 8-11)** and the burial of a man under a small cairn of flints. He had been placed right in the centre of F1, which by now probably looked like

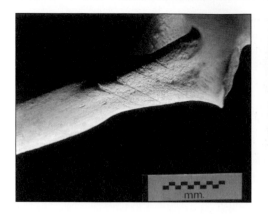
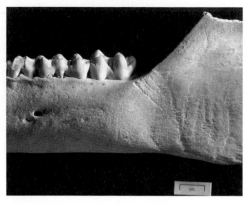

58 Pig bones from the base of the shaft at Monkton Up Wimborne bearing clear butchery marks from a flint knife. (D. Cousins)

an overgrown pond, with his head to the east and feet to the west respecting the axis of the monument. Dated to about 1500 BC, well after the outer pits had been naturally backfilled, the entrances to the monument could only have been detected through gaps in the bank — thus proving that a bank had existed.

Despite this unkempt appearance the site must still have been an important one, and sacred enough to those who buried the man there. His features were also restored during the making of the television programme **(colour plate 10b)**. By the end of the Middle Bronze Age, a small cemetery of at least three burial mounds was constructed within a few yards of the site. One partly excavated during the dig failed to produce any surviving burials, which had probably all been ploughed away. However, we were lucky enough to find pottery in the ditch, which was contemporary with the pottery contained within the final silts of F1. At this stage, well over 2000 years after its construction, the site finally appears to be forgotten.

This site is just one component, albeit a very early one, of a remarkable complex of monuments (*see* **50**) covering some 4km squared and straddling the Cursus. The major influence in the positioning of this complex is undoubtedly the terminal of the Gussage Cursus on Bottlebush Down. As discussed earlier, this most sacred point along the whole monument is where observers would have watched the mid-winter sun set behind the

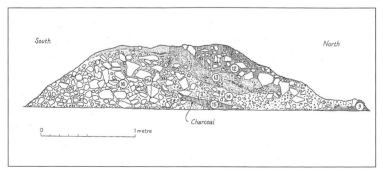

59 Section of the chalk platform, built in four phases at Monkton Up Wimborne

60 *The Knowlton
Circles
ceremonial
complex
(compare with
11). After
RCHME
1975 with
additions (By
permission of
English
Heritage
copyright
reserved)*

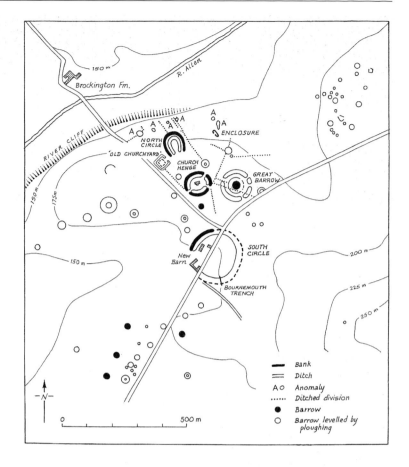

long barrow on Gussage Down. It is therefore no coincidence that the monuments under
discussion lie to the south and west of this point and would all have been within the line
of vision of those witnessing the solstice. Looking at the plan (*see* **50**) it is particularly
interesting to note how the likely earlier monuments (henges, hengi-forms and mortuary
enclosures) all occupy peripheral positions within the main cluster. Although most are at
present unproven through excavation they appear to define to a large extent the
geographical limits of the monument complex. Later round barrow construction is
confined to infilling the area already bounded by sacred parameters.

The currently known distribution of henges on Cranborne Chase clusters in two
groups: those associated with the Cursus and those at Knowlton **(60)**. The two excavated
henges on Wyke Down were discovered through aerial photography. Interestingly, they
were not immediately obvious as such from the air, appearing as ring ditches with no
apparent causeways, so it is likely the number of these monuments in the area has been
greatly underestimated. Indeed recent geophysical survey of six mounds in the Wyke Down
group has shown that half possess causewayed ditches, suggesting Neolithic origins.

The two small henges of Wyke Down 1 and 2 were excavated in 1983-4 and 1996
respectively. The first, WD1 **(61)**, consisted of a ring of closely spaced pits 20m in
diameter, each pit separated by narrow causeways with a three metre entrance gap pointing

85

61 Wyke Down 1 pit circle henge (John Day)

due south to the site of Chalk Pit Field previously discussed. The narrow causeways had eroded allowing soil to fill the interstices giving the impression of a continuous ditch broken by a single entrance. The oval pits varied in depth from 1.35-2m and were about 2m across excepting the western terminal pit that was twice the size of the others. The material excavated from these would have been used to create an external bank, no trace of which survived. After completion a number of objects were placed in the pits which included red deer antler **(62)**, animal bone, flintwork and a few pieces of carved chalk. The pits then started to weather naturally until they half-filled with chalk rubble. Observations during our re-excavation of these pits showed this amount of rubble would have accumulated in less than five years. The sequence shows that at this point small pits were excavated in the top of the rubble and a number of ritual elements included. These differed from those lower down, with no antler or carved chalk present, but instead contained much Grooved Ware pottery and occasional small amounts of human bone. The upper deposits were covered over and subsequently a clayey silt naturally accumulated in the tops of the pits which contained sherds of Late-Style Beaker pottery and pieces of Collared Urn.

Together, these sherds, also found in WD2, indicate later use of the sites which included the digging of a pit in the centre of WD1, dated to 3460±90BP. This activity was probably taking place when the nearby barrow cemetery was under construction. The bulk of the more unusual finds from WD1 are concentrated around the entrance. These include parts of the same Grooved Ware vessel and a transverse arrowhead found in both pits flanking the entrance and a fragment of an internally decorated bowl and a small stone axe of group VIII rock from South Wales in the western terminal pit. A few significant finds from pits at the back of the enclosure suggest that the axis of the monument was carefully marked.

62 Wyke Down 1 henge pit K with antler tools at the base

Wyke Down 2 was smaller, only 12m in diameter, and more irregular having been constructed in two major segments — a semicircular west side and a banana-shaped east side **(46, 63)**. Where the two met at the north end a very narrow degraded causeway was revealed, weathered and perhaps abraded by the passage of feet to a level just below that of the natural chalk. At the southern end a 2m wide causeway gave the henge a SSE axis. This monument too had been constructed by digging a series of oval pits, 10 on the fully excavated western side, with a maximum depth of 1.75m. Unlike WD1, the causeways only survived in the ditch bottoms to a maximum height of 56cm suggesting they had not been left to full height between each pit. Like WD1, the south-western terminal pit revealed a special deposit consisting of a dump of organic rich soil on the base within which was a substantially complete Grooved Ware vessel of unique form **(64, colour plate 12)**. Bearing decorative motifs from all three main styles of Grooved Ware it additionally had an externally decorated base and small pellets applied at intervals to the rim. Carbonised food residues adhered to the inside. On the floor of the north-western terminal pit some scraps of Peterborough Ware were retrieved (an unusual occurrence with Grooved Ware) and on the base of another pit was a small carved chalk ball. No recuts were present and the lower secondary fill contained a rich deposit of Grooved Ware, worked flint and a little daub on the north-west side nearest to the buildings discussed on pages 73-5, suggesting contemporaeity.

63 The Wyke Down henges from the air (Paul Kitching)

The siting of the Wyke Down henges on the east side of the Allen Valley close to its source is undoubtedly significant. The stream links the chalky downlands to the Tertiary soils of the coastal plain and where these two geological areas meet some 3 miles (5km) downstream a very large ceremonial complex of monuments developed in the Neolithic and Bronze Age. Here too, at Knowlton, there is evidence to suggest there were significant natural features already present in the landscape that may have influenced the choice of this place. A substantial Pleistocene river cliff separates the monuments from the valley and stream. Furthermore, a group of at least six anomalous features (*see* **60**) enhances this boundary where it is closest to the main monument complex. These features, as seen from the air, are reminiscent of the shafts already discussed at Down Farm and Pentridge (*see* **21, 24**). Lying very close to the most easterly pair of these features is an oval earthwork that is particularly comparable in form with Neolithic mortuary enclosures, making it likely to be one of the earliest monuments to be constructed in the complex. This juxtapositioning of monuments with natural features is a recurring phenomenon.

The principal components of the Knowlton complex (*see* **60**) consist of four henge monuments and an enormous round mound (the largest in Dorset) which has two concentric ditches surrounding it. The southern circle is the largest in the group being some 230m in diameter. It is bisected by the road to Wimborne, which probably conceals the entrances that have so far failed to show up in any other part of the remainder of the circuit. A small excavation undertaken by Bournemouth University in 1994 cut through the earthwork in the south-eastern quadrant. The ditch was colossal, just under 6m deep and near vertical. Very little survived of the bank after centuries of cultivation but at some stage it had been delimited by two small ditches only 50cm deep. Calculations of the amount of material removed from the ditch revealed it could not have all been contained between these two ditches. It seems likely therefore that the ditches represent a later remodelling of a degraded bank.

At the back of New Barn Farm, which is built within the henge, part of the northern

64 Extraordinary Grooved Ware vessel found in the southern entrance pit of the Wyke Down 2 henge. The externally decorated base is an unique feature

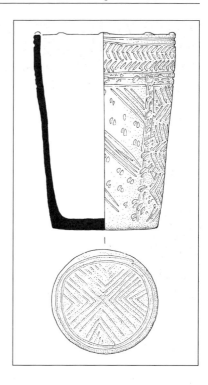

circuit of the earthwork is well preserved and the bank width can be measured at some 12m. Lying 140m to the north is the centre circle. This earthwork is one of the best preserved of its kind in the country and receives protection under English Heritage guardianship. It is occupied by the ruin of a Norman church and its attendant graveyard defined by a low bank. The church sits on a low mound and one wonders whether this mound was an original Neolithic feature? The henge is roughly oval in plan with a maximum width of just over 100m. The bank is up to 2m high and the ditch over 1m deep appears rather irregular, interrupted by a number of causeways. Today there are three entrances, although only the eastern one appears to be original. Just to the north of this monument, badly degraded by ploughing, is a smaller circle with a wide entrance to the south east and a roughly square earthwork known as 'old churchyard'. The latter is likely to be another henge as it has a causeway to the north-east aligned on the entrance to the northern circle although unusually its bank lies on the inside.

Due east of the centre circle, covered in trees, is the great mound still surviving to a height of 6.5m. Two concentric ditches surround it, one within 5m of the mound and the outer, segmented ditch, set some 30m distant from it **(colour plate 11)**. It is possible that this outer ditch, over 10m in diameter, is in fact a fifth henge within which the mound was constructed. Supporting this hypothesis are some aerial photographs that clearly reveal traces of an external bank. A rescue excavation in 1958 (Field 1962), following a pipe trench which cut the ditch, uncovered a profile apparently less than 2m deep which is admittedly rather un-henge like. However, bearing in mind the causewayed nature of the ditch, the profile could vary significantly around its circuit.

Nothing is known of this mound but similar combinations of henges and large mounds are known in other parts of the country — notably at Arbor Low in Derbyshire, Marden in Wiltshire and the most extreme example of all Silbury Hill and the Avebury complex. The large Neolithic round mound Duggleby Howe on the Yorkshire Wolds is now known to lie at the centre of a surrounding causewayed enclosure (Selkirk 1980). Silbury Hill is known to date from 3000 BC and it is likely that the other mounds are of broadly similar date.

Surrounding the remarkable group at Knowlton are numerous round barrows, now mostly only visible from the air, including several of two phase construction. Using the great mound as a centre point of a 1km wide circle, around 60 barrows are now known within this area and numbers are likely to increase with future aerial survey. Some seem to form an avenue (*see* **60**) approaching the site from the south-west. The greater percentage of these mounds are likely to be of Bronze Age origin attesting to the continuing importance this place held for succeeding generations. Indeed, the construction of the church within the central henge in the twelfth century **(colour plate 13)**, 0.5km from the medieval settlement, is an eloquent reminder of continuing pagan beliefs and the clergy's attempt to integrate them with Christianity.

We have seen how the construction of the Dorset Cursus created a huge spinal earthwork, stamping the landscape through which it crossed with special sacred status. Once built it acted as a focal point, and sites like those found on Down Farm reveal increasing evidence of more sustained settlement and an expanding population through the third millennium BC. The sheer range and number of smaller ceremonial earthworks, created to embellish and enhance the Cursus line, are evidence of this consolidation. The discoveries made on Wyke Down suggest such monuments are only one component of an increasingly ordered and settled landscape.

6 Barrows, graves and hierarchy:
Early Bronze Age pomp and prestige

Towards the very end of the third millennium BC, distinctive Beaker pottery starts to appear in the archaeological record. During its period of use single, usually crouched, burials beneath round barrows become the norm. Occasionally accompanying these burials are some of the first metal items of gold, copper and bronze to appear in this country. Archaeologists are still unsure as to how much the presence of these new items is a result of immigration of people, particularly from the Rhineland where directly comparable material is widespread, or, as is more likely to be the case, new ideas travelling across the channel with increased trading links. From what we have already seen of the emerging élite in the last chapter it would not have taken long for them to adopt this new 'package', as it has been called, in order to enhance their status.

The power the bright new metals and fine pottery gave to those who owned and controlled them cannot be overestimated. It therefore should be no surprise to us that many of the earthwork symbols of power of the old order should be remodelled and embellished during this phase. Indeed, the first stone setting at Stonehenge can be attributed to this period. It involved the colossal task of quarrying over 60 four-ton blocks in south-west Wales and transporting them some 137 miles (220km) to this most sacred of sites on Salisbury Plain. Such an undertaking not only broadcast the power of the new order but also enabled those who erected them to inherit cumulative status from an already ancient place of ceremony and ritual. This phenomenon is also well documented on Cranborne Chase where a number of sites are shown by excavation to have been altered and additions made. Most noteworthy of all is at Hambledon Hill where occasional parts of the causewayed enclosure ditch were recut down to the original base. This latter segment was associated with sherds of Beaker pottery. By this stage the ditch would have been entirely filled and even slightly mounded by the final Neolithic deposits, prompting Roger Mercer who dug the site to remark that we should perhaps add field archaeology to the list of skills practised by these people! The Dorset Cursus complex also reveals evidence of use at this time. The secondary silts of the ditch contained Beaker sherds and the smaller of the two long barrows at the Thickthorn terminal had three burials, two with Beakers, inserted into it, an unambiguous sign of re-dedication.

The Wor Barrow burial complex (*see* **32**) also comes to a surprisingly complete end with Pitt Rivers' discovery of a crouched Beaker burial only a few metres south of the long barrow. He located this grave through the technique of 'bosing' which requires the methodical thumping of old grassland with a sledge hammer and the noting of the different resonance produced by major changes in soil depth. This primitive predecessor of geophysical techniques was used by the General with great success on a number of his

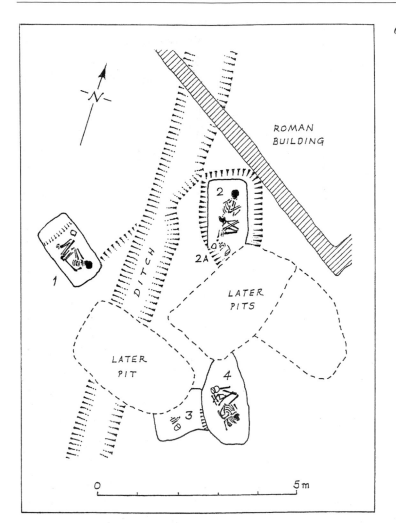

65 Barton Hill Beaker graves Tarrant Hinton (Courtesy Priest's House Museum, Wimborne)

excavations. The burial at Wor Barrow is one example of an increasing number of Beaker graves discovered with no trace of a mound or encircling ditch. In Susan Gibbs' Walk at Rushmore, Pitt Rivers found a further grave covered by a low mound but with no ditch. It seems likely that a number of these burials were provided with only slight mounds which did not require quarry ditches. Later ploughing could remove all traces of such small mounds and leave these apparently flat graves to be found fortuitously during large-scale excavations.

One such example was discovered by Pitt Rivers at the Romano-British village at Rotherley, but the most interesting was a group found during the excavations of a Roman villa at Barton Hill, Tarrant Hinton (Keen 1976). Here four graves were uncovered which contained the remains of five individuals **(65)**. Two of these had been badly disturbed by Roman pits but enough survived to suggest the group represents a small family cemetery which could have been covered by a small mound some 7m in diameter of which no trace survived. The finding of Beakers in all but one of the graves, and a necklace consisting of

66 *Oakley Down barrow cemetery from Colt Hoare's Ancient Wiltshire. Compare with* **14**

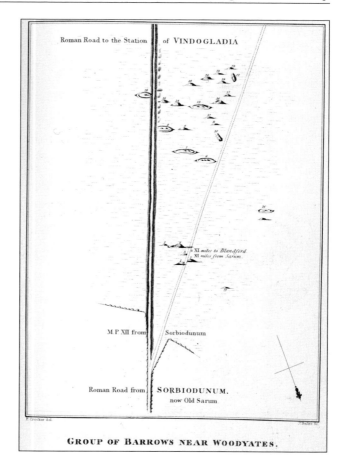

GROUP OF BARROWS NEAR WOODYATES.

29 exquisitely perforated shale beads only 4mm in diameter, indicated that the group was of high status. Furthermore, additional evidence showed that bronze or copper items, probably knives, had once accompanied two of the individuals. The only traces of these objects were tell-tale green stains on some of the vertebrae of a skeleton disturbed in Roman times — perhaps evidence of an early antiquarian excavation. Sadly, another metal item partially uncovered was stolen during the course of the excavation. Evidence of a possible nearby settlement was indicated by two pits containing domestic assemblages some 70m to the north-east of the graves.

One of the highest-status graves in the area was excavated by Colt Hoare in a large bowl barrow (no 9) on Oakley Down **(66)**. This barrow seems to represent a shift in the cemetery focus at Wor Barrow discussed earlier, to a new location some 600m to the east, overlooking the springhead of the River Crane. The grave revealed a crouched inhumation together with an astonishingly fine array of grave goods consisting of a flat bronze dagger, bronze awl, shale or jet button and pulley ring, and four superbly flaked barbed and tanged flint arrowheads. It is tempting to see this high-status grave as that of a local chief whose burial became the focal point for the development of a major cemetery during the remaining part of the Early Bronze Age, widely referred to in the literature as the 'Wessex culture' (Piggott 1938). The key features of this transition are the replacement of Beakers with new forms of urns and the gradual adoption of cremation as the dominant burial rite.

Barrow cemeteries

The clustering of large numbers of barrows close to the Cursus clearly reflects its continued importance well into the second millennium BC. A large percentage of the round barrows and ring ditches (usually flattened round barrows) lie within 1km of the monument with two major cemeteries extending over the adjacent Wyke and Oakley Downs. Paradoxically, very few barrows were actually built within the Cursus itself leading to the belief that it marked some form of exclusion zone. I know of only six barrows/ring ditches in two groups included within its course. On Wyke Down four barrows are built in a line some 250m long which share the monuments axis. These lie only 500m down slope from the Bottlebush terminal and are purposefully placed to reinforce and parallel the mid-winter alignment. The other two ring ditches lie on the west side of Gussage Down.

Little is known of the plough-damaged Wyke Down group **(67)** but our knowledge of Oakley is much greater due to excavations, which took place almost 200 years ago. This fine barrow group was first noted by the great field antiquary William Stukely, who on an excursion to the area described how the Roman road (Ackling Dyke) cut through one of the disc barrows **(66)**. This astute piece of observation showed the barrow to pre-date the Roman era, an important discovery at such an early stage of study into British antiquities. However, the contents of the barrow itself would remain undisclosed for a few decades further until the work of one of the most famous of all early antiquarian explorers.

Sir Richard Colt Hoare (1758-1838) **(68a)** was a man of keen intellect who inherited considerable wealth from his family's banking business. On returning from the 'grand tour' of European centres of culture and learning he was fired with a desire to explore and describe the wealth of prehistoric remains which lay within, and close to, his Wiltshire estate of Stourhead. Fortunately he had made the acquaintance of William Cunnington **(68b)**, a man with a similar desire, and the two joined forces to form a formidable and lasting partnership. Although Cunnington was on a considerably lower social plain than Hoare, the two formed an enduring friendship until Cunnington's untimely death in 1810. Together they planned campaigns of fieldwork and excavations that consisted of initial reconnaissance and then excavation of the many burial mounds dotted across the downs. The examination of monuments was not exactly new, but one of their unique innovations was the production of accurate site plans — not only of barrow cemeteries but of less obvious earthworks — many of which were the remains of former settlement sites. To do this Hoare employed Phillip Crocker, a professional surveyor seconded from the Ordnance Survey, whose accurate plans have proved to be of lasting value (*see* **66**). The major excavation effort was concentrated on the burial mounds they encountered, particularly those around Stonehenge which formed an especially dense concentration. Over a comparatively short period of years 465 burial mounds were examined, most of which lay in southern Wiltshire but with a few in Dorset. Those in Dorset are of particular interest to us because they include the cemetery on Oakley Down.

The main cluster of barrows here consists of a group of some 20 mounds with a

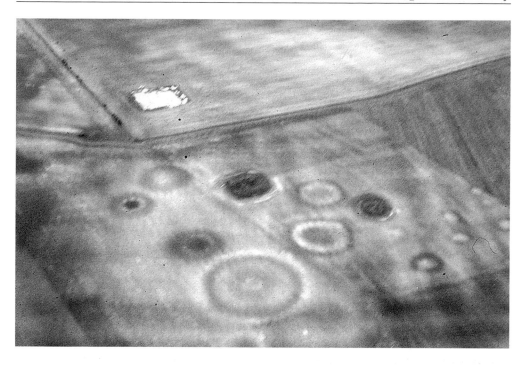

67 *Aerial view of the Wyke Down barrow cemetery. The Wyke Down 1 henge can be seen in course of excavation near the top left hand corner*

further 10 or so in the near vicinity, all of which were examined by the dynamic duo. The first barrow to have been built at the site, number 9, has already been described but its opening by Colt Hoare's party appeared to unleash the dead occupant's wrath! The description of the occasion in Hoare's sumptuous two volume work *Ancient Wiltshire* is worth repeating:

> The opening of this barrow was attended by so many awful circumstances, and gave birth to so beautiful and truly descriptive a poem, by my friend the Rev William Lisle Bowles, who attended our operations, that it will ever be remembered both with horror and pleasure by those who were present. During the tremendous storm of thunder and lightning by which my friend and companion Mr Fenton, my surveyor Mr Phillip Crocker, & co; & co; were surprised, our only place of refuge was the barrow, which had been excavated to a considerable depth; the lightning flashed upon our spades and iron instruments, and the large flints poured down upon us from the summit so forcibly, that we were obliged to quit our hiding place, and abide the pelting of the pitiless storm upon the bleak and unsheltered down. Mr. Bowles took leave of us the same evening, and the next morning sent me the following beautiful and spirited poem, so truly descriptive of the awful scene we had so lately witnessed.

68 a Sir Richard Colt Hoare.

One verse will suffice here to give a flavour:

> 'Let me, let me sleep again;
> Thus methought in feeble strain.
> Plain'd from it's disturbed bed
> The spirit of the mighty dead'

Hoare and Cunnington's opening techniques either consisted of digging a shaft down from the summit (of the larger mounds) or in smaller examples of trenching from one side to the other, effectively cutting through the centre of the mound. In this way they were able to locate all the centrally placed primary burials at the site and gather the rich haul of grave goods. The human remains were generally reinterred without much study. On one occasion, however, commenting on the fine condition of a skeleton just uncovered, Hoare remarked: 'the long bones could survive being thrown a considerable distance without breaking'. Perhaps due reverence was not always accorded to the ancient dead!

A few of the mounds on Oakley Down are of a particular type known as disc barrows **(colour plate 14)**. These consist of a very small central tump or tumps which are then encircled by a ditch and an external bank set at some distance away. It is generally accepted that the burials found in these mounds are of high-status females and they are often furnished with fine grave goods. Several necklaces of amber and faience were uncovered including one formed of over 100 beads. Ceramic finds included decorated accessory cups

68 b William Cunnington

and a magnificent Collared Urn **(69)**. The larger mounds of the bowl and bell barrows, probably housing high-status male graves, contained further wealthy finds including exquisitely crafted bronze daggers, bone pins and further beads of amber and shale **(colour plate 15)**. Badly fragmented vessels appear to have been left behind in the opening holes, sometimes together with skeletal remains as I witnessed some years ago whilst helping on a re-excavation of mound 23. In this case within the central burial pit were fragments of a Collared Urn, cremated remains of at least two individuals and a lead plaque stamped WC 1804! This latter object can be seen today in The Priest's House Museum in Wimborne.

Although round barrows are generally regarded as mounds to cover the grave of one high-status individual there is increasing evidence to show that graves are often reopened and further burials made even sometimes before the barrow was constructed. Once a mound was built, it was frequently dug through to place further human remains either in the central burial pit or at other points. Sometimes an initial mound would be enlarged by the digging of a further ditch or ditches. Barrows of more than one phase often show up on aerial photographs as concentric rings (*see* **colour plate 11**). Barrows became focal points for later secondary burials cut into either the mounds or the ditches and were used even up until the Anglo-Saxon period (*see* **80**). A number of the latter were revealed during Hoare's excavations, as we shall see later.

The Oakley Down barrows and similar clusters like them probably represent wealthy clan cemeteries where the most important members of society were interred. The burial clusters developed over several hundred years and were striking reminders to those

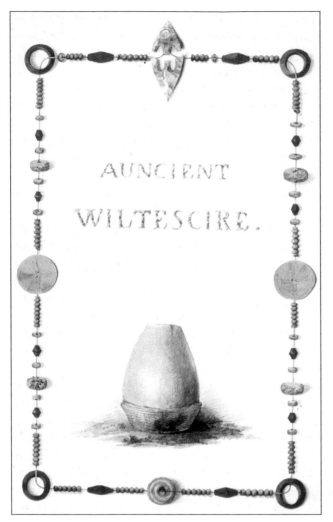

Frontispiece from Ancient Wiltshire. The large Collared Urn was found during the excavations on Oakley Down. (Wiltshire Archaeological & Natural History Society)

present in the landscape of the influential power of those families who were placed there. Occasional single or small groups of mounds appear to represent individual family cemeteries of lesser status. Just one such cemetery was found on Down Farm and took the unusual form of a 'pond barrow'.

Pond barrows are a particularly uncommon form of Bronze Age monument. Instead of the usual mound a pond like hollow is excavated and the material removed is usually piled up around the perimeter to form an external circular bank. They are normally associated with large 'Wessex'-type barrow groups and their distribution is practically restricted to that area. Very little is known about them as so few have been scientifically examined, and those that have show a great variation in lay-out.

The Down Farm example revealed itself as a dark patch in the soil during fieldwalking. I thought at the time it might be a man-made pond associated with a nearby Middle Bronze Age settlement then being excavated. Later, excavations revealed the true nature of this remarkable site with the uncovering of a well-defined circular feature some 19m in diameter **(70)**. This feature contained fills that only survived to a maximum depth of 15cm after heavy truncation by ploughing. The vulnerability of this type of monument to the destructive effects of cultivation cannot be over emphasised and it is therefore likely to be under-represented in the archaeological record.

Around the northern and eastern periphery of the barrow, both inside and outside the dished area, burials were encountered. Eight cremations were found in total, five within urns **(colour plate 17),** containing the remains of eight adults and three infants. Three of these were placed in elaborate funnel shaped pits, one of which was accompanied by a bronze and two bone awls. In addition there were five infant inhumations ranging in age from near-natal to two years. Two of them were provided with Food Vessels and the two-year-old by a group of rounded flints, which were almost certainly playthings. Four animal burials were also recorded, two domestic cows placed some 5m from the eastern and western edges of the hollow respectively and two sheep, one badly disturbed by ploughing, on the northern and southern rim of the feature. Lines drawn between these two sets of burials cross at the centre of the hollow where a setting of four postholes were found, one containing a broken Food Vessel. Leading from the eastern group of burials, three large postholes continued the partly linear arrangement of the eastern cemetery **(70)**. The axis of this alignment not only led straight to the centre of the monument but also repeated that of the Cursus which lies only 35m away. The complex layout of this monument with its references to the Cursus, built some 1800 years earlier, is a clear statement of the continuing role it had to play in the lives of succeeding generations.

From the recently excavated examples of pond barrows we can see that burial was certainly part of their function but by no means the only one, as shown by their great complexity (eg. Atkinson et al 1951). For example there is a tendency for burials to be located around the edge of the monument, sometimes placed under the bank, leaving the dished area relatively free of features. In this form there appears to be a connection between pond barrows and the smaller henge monuments such as those at Wyke Down. Both create sacred circular areas where ceremonial activity could take place and both involved the placing of human and animal remains around the perimeter as part of the rituals. It should perhaps come as no surprise that Wyke Down 1 henge showed clear evidence of reuse in the Early Bronze Age with a pit being dug at the centre and sherds of Collared Urn being found in the top of the perimeter pits. The reuse of Wyke Down is likely to be contemporary with the growth of the nearby barrow cemetery, the location of which was no doubt influenced by the pre-existing henge complex.

Settlement evidence

Evidence for settlements in this period is rare at a regional level. The national picture is not much better, with only a handful of known house sites. However, flint scatters that contain a reasonable percentage of finished tools distinctive to the period are reasonably widespread. These forms in the main consist of small well made round scrapers, scale or invasively flaked knives, and barbed and tanged arrowheads (*see* **42, nos 8-11**). Flintwork of this type is found in the area but almost universally amongst much earlier scatters, which makes the accurate plotting of individual foci almost impossible. Scatters of this kind represent settlement locations but excavations in general reveal few if any features

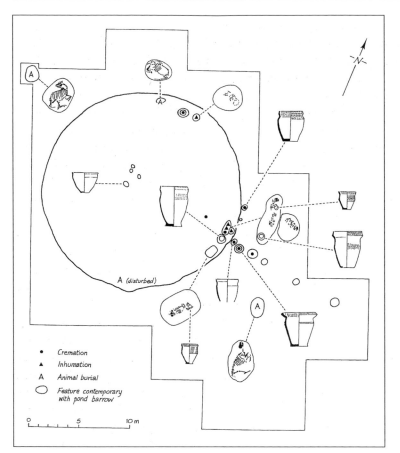

70 Down Farm pond barrow

•   Cremation

▲   Inhumation

A   Animal burial

◯   Feature contemporary with pond barrow

below ground. If stake-built houses were the norm, and this seems to be the case where conditions have allowed preservation, few would survive the normal degradation caused by arable agriculture. However, just because houses were stake-built does not mean they were insubstantial. Replication such as that undertaken at the nearby Ancient Technology Centre at Cranborne (Keen 1996) has shown that very strong houses could be constructed of stakes, which do not require the digging of holes deep into the underlying subsoil, thus leaving little evidence of their former presence.

Occasionally Early Bronze Age horizons yield domestic material that can be found preserved within earlier features. Such a case is provided by the sections through the Dorset Cursus that showed distinct Beaker levels towards the top of the ditch. Analysis of the snails from these levels revealed a massive increase in open country species, suggesting renewed clearance and farming taking place within the immediate area. Further evidence for this is provided by the pit group underlying the pond barrow discussed below.

A particularly rich Early Bronze Age horizon occurred in the shaft in Fir Tree Field (see chapter 3). The penultimate fill consisted of deliberate chalk rubble packing which may represent a symbolic capping to the feature. Immediately below this a few sherds of Beaker were recovered. Gradual compaction eventually left a shallow depression at the top, which slowly accumulated a fill, rich in Beaker debris. Over 150 sherds were discovered with a flint industry typical of this period. Traces of a substantial domestic presence were revealed when an extensive area around the shaft was stripped (*see* **45**). A post-built roundhouse was uncovered which produced a sherd of Beaker from one of the postholes, and a nearby cluster of three large pits contained rich accumulations of pottery, animal bone and flintwork. One of the pits had a small hole cut into its base, which contained a large portion of a very fine Beaker indicating a ritual element. Further sherds of the same Beaker were found in another of the pits revealing contemporaneous filling.

A similar horizon was discovered in the large central pit at Monkton Up Wimborne (see previous chapter). This level was formed during a long period of stabilisation when vegetation grew thick in the abandoned pit and is clearly dated by a few sherds of Beaker and barbed and tanged arrowheads found within it. Around this time the crouched body of a man was placed in the overgrown pit and covered by a cairn of natural flints.

As long ago as the 1890s Pitt Rivers had revealed a few traces of an earlier settlement underlying the Middle Bronze Age enclosure on Martin Down. A number of pits including two with Beaker pottery were uncovered together with further sherds incorporated into later features. Other examples of sites like this, yielding only the deeper elements of settlement foci, have already been noted from Tarrant Hinton and underlying the pond barrow in Fir Tree Field (Barrett et al 1991). This latter site produced a particularly large group of pits, 11 in all, covering an area of about 12x6m. Several had been partly truncated by the excavation of the later earthwork and the rest lay beyond its north-western edge. Domestic debris was obtained from most of the pits and included pottery, worked flint and animal bone, One pit contained a badly crushed but substantially complete Beaker within which was a small plain bowl. Nearby on the floor of another pit a lower jaw of a pig had been placed, suggesting ritual elements to some of the fillings. Two radiocarbon samples produced dates in the later third millennium BC (see Appendix).

As we have seen, traces of earlier Bronze Age settlement are not uncommon in the area, but in the next chapter we shall see that coherent settlement plans with clear buildings only become widespread during a period of dramatic reorganisation, beginning in the latter half of the Bronze Age.

7 Farms, fields and boundaries:
beginnings of an ordered agricultural landscape

The Later Bronze Age consists of an earlier phase, conventionally Middle Bronze Age and characterised by Deverel-Rimbury ceramics (including Barrel, Bucket and Globular Urns), and a later phase producing post-Deverel-Rimbury ceramic forms. As we have seen, the Neolithic and Early Bronze Age are dominated by funerary and ceremonial sites with few domestic settlements. This pattern has almost certainly more to do with survival and present-day retrieval methods than an absolute absence of domestic activity. One problem is that earlier settlement areas without earthworks bounding them are unlikely to be found except by chance. Equally the few shallow pits, post and stakeholes which survived centuries of subsequent intensive agriculture rarely produce coherent settlement plans. The sort of sites we should expect have already been seen to exist with the numerous incidental discoveries described in the previous two chapters. These finds represent the deeper elements within settlement areas that have survived the ravages of later agriculture and have been recorded on numerous sites throughout Britain. How many excavation reports, based around much later sites, start with a description of a scatter of Neolithic and Bronze Age features? We no longer need to give a mystified shrug to the question, 'Where are all the Neolithic and Early Bronze Age settlements?' They were there all the time but we failed to recognise them for what they were.

By the Middle Bronze Age however, population increase and the subsequent pressure for land led to the deliberate enclosing of settlement areas and the creation of well-defined intensive field systems. Earlier slighter systems are unlikely to survive although occasionally fragments of these have been observed underlying Middle Bronze Age systems, exemplified by South Lodge. Evidence from recent excavations at South Lodge and Down Farm (Barrett et al 1991) have shown that both these sites started as unenclosed settlements and that enclosure was a later development. If it had not been for these enclosures it is unlikely that these sites would have ever been discovered — because of their excellent preservation it is worth examining them in some detail.

Settlements
During his work on Cranborne Chase General Pitt Rivers excavated what we now know to be three partly enclosed settlements. Two of these, Martin Down and South Lodge, survived as earthwork enclosures and a third, Angle Ditch, was located by 'bosing' (p91) close to Wor Barrow. The range of domestic debris uncovered in the ditches and banks of these earthworks was impressive, although surprisingly few internal features were found. This prompted the General to visualise these sites as compounds for the management of

livestock, particularly cattle, although he noted the debris in the ditches, 'imply residence of some kind'. Furthermore, surface trenching inside the Angle Ditch produced sufficient debris for him to postulate, 'a place of residence had probably existed', but 'no trace of any habitation could be found'.

We know from re-excavation at South Lodge that the General excavated quickly in narrow successive trenches. Sometimes this trenching was over-zealous and removed part of the underlying bedrock. In all probability the revealed surface would not have been very clean and therefore recognition of small features such as postholes would have been difficult at best. The material from the next trench would be used to fill the previous one and work progressed in this way across the site producing only a small area to be seen for a short period at any given time. Bearing this in mind it is not surprising that smaller features were usually missed, particularly at South Lodge where the bedrock was badly decayed by water and tree root action. However, where better surfaces were uncovered postholes were occasionally recognised, as at the Romano-British village at Rotherley where several four-post settings were revealed.

Martin Down and the Grim's Ditch complex

Our description of the enclosures begins by looking at the largest: the site of Martin Down. Covering nearly a hectare and with a ditch 3m deep (**71**), this enclosure was clearly an important site. The ditch consists of three segments: a 'C'-shaped western side, surrounding half the site; a right-angled section defining the eastern corner; and a kinked length to the north. Two clear entrances are defined on the south-east and north-east sides with an odd looking 50m gap on the north-west side. This may have been closed by a fence, such as the fence revealed at Down Farm (*see* **73**), although it is surprising that Pitt Rivers did not find it, clearly stating that 'no trace of any such work could be seen'. Few internal features were found, leaving Pitt Rivers to conclude that it was probably used for the management of cattle. However, this seems unlikely given the fact that over 60% of the recovered pottery came from the interior as well as quantities from the buried soil under the bank. The latter is particularly interesting as it proves conclusively that there had been significant pre-enclosure activity. As we shall see later, this was not the only time that the General had difficulty in explaining apparently contradictory evidence.

According to recent studies it has also been suggested that the site occupies a significant position marking the edge of a boundary. For example, Bowen (1991) has argued persuasively that the line of Bokerley Dyke, which is still the county boundary, overlies a much earlier Bronze Age boundary. He notes that the linear ditch system, very extensive to the east, comes to a dramatic halt at this line. Part of this system known as the Grim's Ditch seems to form an enormous 'enclosure' (Piggott 1944). Delineating an area of some 11x4km, it comprises a series of lengths of bank and ditch that are sometimes of rather different form. At the western end, close to Woodyates, a number of the ditches come together to form a funnelled entrance into the 'enclosure' which if not originally conceived as a single entity may have become one. Further ditches in this area appear to form some kind of internal partitioning within which lies the Martin Down enclosure. This careful placement suggests the site had an important function controlling access to and management within the great 'enclosure'. Ellison (1980b) in her studies of Middle

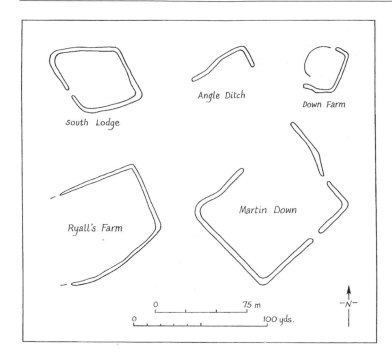

71 Outline plans of five Middle Bronze Age enclosures on Cranborne Chase

Bronze Age ceramics notes that the site is at the edge of two fine ware-style zones and the site may have also been a focus for exchange and redistribution.

At the south-eastern corner of the Grim's Ditch 'enclosure' a number of ditches, including two which form part of it, appear to spring from a nodal point which is occupied by the impressive multivallate hillfort of Whitsbury. Although unproven at this site, it is likely that the hillfort is constructed over the linear ditches and may overlie a significant later Bronze Age site which could have been the eastern equivalent to Martin Down.

To summarise, the Grim's Ditch complex defines a large tract of land whose primary purpose is perhaps the containment and management of livestock on a grand scale. We shall now turn to the sites in the west and south of this area where evidence indicates evolving field systems and enclosures associated with the establishment of a well-defined mixed farming economy.

The site of South Lodge was selected for re-examination by Richard Bradley and John Barrett as part of the Cranborne Chase project. The transfer of the Cranborne Chase material from Farnham to Salisbury Museum in 1977 provided the opportunity to re-evaluate Pitt Rivers' work, not just from his publications but from surviving records and finds from one of the former excavated sites. South Lodge was selected as it potentially contained the most complete range of structural elements one could hope for: a likely settlement enclosure, including a portion of the interior unexamined by Pitt Rivers, a cemetery and surrounding field system (72). Pitt Rivers' excavations had totally cleared the bulk of the bank of the earthwork and most of the interior except for one small area left untrenched because of growing trees. It was this area which was selected first for investigation to see what, if anything, had survived of the original land surface. It soon became clear, despite the badly eroded surface, that features were indeed preserved. A

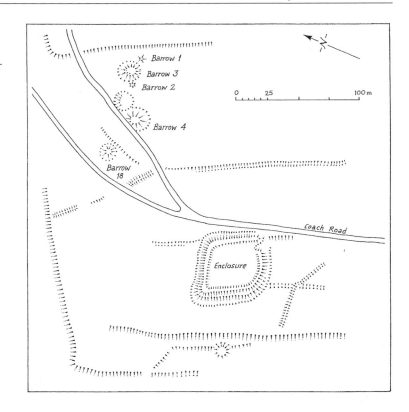

72 *South Lodge Bronze Age landscape* (After Barrett et al 1991)

roundhouse some 5m in diameter was uncovered containing a pit with a partial skeleton of a small cow. After this initial success it was decided to strip the bulk of the interior of the enclosure. This resulted in the discovery of a further, more substantial roundhouse, scatters of other postholes, pits and a low mound of burnt flints. The latter accumulation was probably the result of 'trough' cooking in a nearby elongated pit. This method, well documented elsewhere, involved the placing of a wooden trough in a pit or gully which was then filled with water. Stones were then heated in a nearby fire and dropped into the trough so that food could be boiled. The troughs were generally large enough for whole animal carcasses to be cooked in this way.

A small portion of bank was sectioned on the eastern side of the enclosure showing that underneath the nineteenth-century spoil there was only a very slight hump which had not been constructed with rubble from the ditch. This was also shown to be true of the western side. However, on the northern and southern sides there is evidence that the ditches were cut and quickly backfilled, deliberately burying at one point a large Barrel Urn that had been placed on the floor of the ditch. Emerging from the corners of the enclosure on the western and eastern sides were lynchets of an earlier field system first recorded by one of Pitt Rivers' former assistants, H.S. Toms, in 1925. The 'bank' revealed in the section was in fact a continuation of these lynchets which predated the digging of the ditch, implying some form of open settlement prior to enclosure. Some internal evidence suggested that two fields had been removed by the construction of the enclosure ditch. At Down Farm further evidence for pre-enclosure settlement was uncovered.

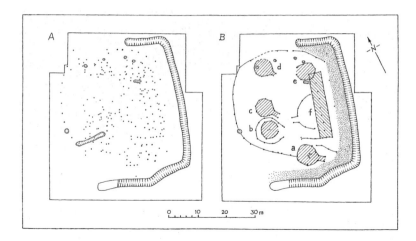

73 Down Farm Middle Bronze Age settlement. A — all Middle Bronze Age features B — structural interpretation

The enclosure here **(73)** consisted of a ditch on three sides with a fence forming the fourth. A 4m strip relatively devoid of features, which lay immediately behind the ditch, provided evidence for an internal bank. Inside the enclosure were a number of structures consisting of six roundhouses, a large rectangular building, a possible four-post structure and a series of short fence lines. Interestingly, five of the six roundhouses had their entrances aligned to the south-east. This orientation conforms to a pattern noted throughout Britain at this time and it is something we will return to later in the chapter.

It was clear that not all the buildings were contemporary and at least two predated the construction of the enclosure. In order to understand the sequence we need to make a number of detailed observations, which can be followed on the accompanying plans **(73)**. For example, house A was too close to the ditch to have post-dated this feature and the ditch at this point also kinks in a way that suggests it was deliberately avoiding the structure. We must remember that the circle of posts does not represent the outer wall of these buildings but the inner structural ring. The outer stake-built wall, traces of which are unlikely to survive, would have lain about another two metres beyond this ring. Another early structure is house B (inner ring) which is cut by a shallow gully which in turn is cut by a posthole of the perimeter fence proving it predates the enclosure. The outer ring of B is likely to be a replacement for the inner ring and is too close to house C for them to have been contemporary; this suggests that it too belongs to the earlier open phase of settlement. Enclosure then takes place with the building of three further roundhouses: C **(74)**, which replaces B (outer ring), and D and E which oppose each other inside the gateway on the north side and a yard butted on to the back of the bank. The latest phase **(colour plate 18)** sees the construction of the large rectangular building F which required the demolition of E and the yard. This most unusual building **(75)** over 18m long appears to be divided into two parts. The north-eastern part is demarcated by extra postholes forming a partition wall. Higher phosphate readings from this area of the building suggest that this part may have been used for housing animals. The remaining part of the building could have been used for human habitation and storage. Indeed, very few pits were found suggesting the use of other methods of storage. This apparent division of the building is very similar to that evident in Medieval long houses. Recently a striking

74 Middle Bronze Age roudhouse C, Down Farm

parallel for this building has been recovered from the floodplain of the Great Ouse in Cambridgeshire (Evans and Knight 1996). It too was set within a 'C'-shaped ditched compound and had replaced an earlier roundhouse. The eastern end also had many more postholes suggesting that, like Down Farm, this end was used for a different purpose than the rest of the building.

Analysis of the finds from Down Farm gives us some idea of the type of farming practised at this time (Barrett et al 1991b). Surviving animal bones show cattle were the most common species at 55%, with sheep second in abundance at 39% and much smaller amounts of pig (2.2%), dog (1.6%) and the remainder made up of wild species. The age at death percentages for the cattle and sheep suggest that cattle were principally kept for milk production and the sheep for meat. Surviving plant remains were scarce but included wheat, barley and a number of arable weeds including fat hen, which was probably used as a vegetable. A carbonised tuber of onion couch shows that even then farmers were plagued with this invasive grass weed. Sarsen and greensandstone rubbers testify to grain processing. Both stones occur quite often in the local geology. The nearest source of greensandstone, for example, lies in the Blackmoor Vale some ten miles distant.

Further light was thrown on the procurement of this material by Pitt Rivers who investigated the previously enigmatic site at Pen Pits on the Dorset/Somerset border near Zeals (Pitt Rivers 1884). His excavations proved the irregular earthworks were the remains of former quarry workings to extract the greensandstone for quern manufacture. The area he dug produced evidence of a Romano-British date, but occasional finds of earlier material and the vast area covered by the workings suggest that the quarrying probably started much earlier. Bronze, although widespread at this time, was highly valued and only a few items have been found on settlement sites. At South Lodge, for instance, a bronze spearhead, two razors and part of a bracelet were found in the ditch. Axe marks were found in the chalk of Angle Ditch and, remarkably, the broken axe was discovered discarded nearby. Flint was still the most important raw material for tool making and it was used extensively but with much less skill than in preceding periods. Consequently the resulting products were often very poorly made. It seems the only basic requirement was

to produce a flake with an edge suitable for cutting. These flakes are often very thick, have large bulbs and terminate in hinge fractures. When found in large numbers during fieldwalking their presence is most helpful in detecting settlement areas, especially in places where pottery is unlikely to survive in the ploughsoil. Finished tool forms are very few **(76)** and comprise scrapers, borers, knives and pounders/pestles, the latter probably used both for making and re-dressing the querns and rubbers as well as for actually grinding seeds into flour. During this period evidence for craftwork is sparse, due mainly to the poor survival of organic materials. Nevertheless there is spinning and weaving equipment **(77)** which implies developed textile and cloth working. After worked flint, pottery sherds are the most common artefacts retrieved on these sites. For the most part they consist of fragments of coarse ware vessels of bucket and barrel form often decorated with finger tipped applied cordons as well as fine ware globular forms with incised or furrowed decoration on the shoulder. Much the same forms of pots were used for burial, as we shall see later in this chapter, suggesting that exclusive forms of funerary vessels were abandoned in the later Bronze Age.

   The downland slope position of these settlement sites is fairly typical of the Wessex area, although there is increasing evidence for intensive use of river valleys as well. Large

76 *Middle Bronze Age flint tools from the Down Farm settlement — pounders 1 & 3, borer 2, scrapers 4 & 5and knife 6. (J. Richards)*

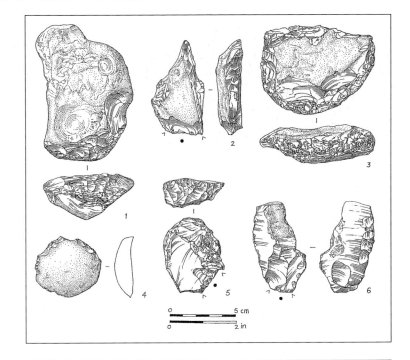

77 *Middle Bronze Age bone tools from the Down Farm settlement. Gouges/weaving shuttles a-c, awl d and antler ferrule e*

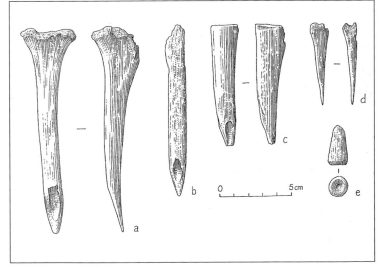

spreads of burnt flint are often found in these areas and when dated invariably turn out to be later Bronze Age. The bulk of these spreads probably represent debris created during 'trough' cooking which we discussed earlier, but added to this there is some evidence for industrial activities. An indication of this new complexity comes from Everley water meadows near Stourpaine where Roger Mercer (1984) found a mould for a socketed bronze axe amongst deposits of this kind, partially filling a former course of the River Iwerne. At Gussage St Michael and Monkton Up Wimborne intense fieldwork in former meadows has located similar deposits in the Gussage and Allen valleys, including one in

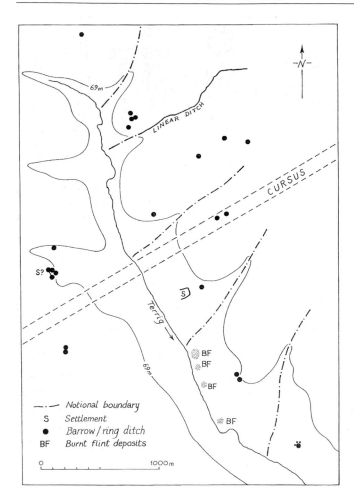

78 *Bronze Age features and notional boundaries in the Upper Gussage valley*

the latter over 100m in length. At Gussage, next to the former meandering course of the brook **(78)**, clear evidence for bronze working has been retrieved. An area of some 20x30m contained much casting waste, broken artefacts, and a complete socketed axe **(79)**. Further finds of bronze artefacts, including the tip of a gouge broken in manufacture and still containing part of its sand casting plug, stretch the distribution of finds to well over a kilometre in this part of the valley. The low-lying land, subject to flooding, was probably used sporadically for the domestic and industrial purposes we have just discussed as well as providing a wide range of natural resources including reeds, willow, wildfowl, fish and of course, water. Settlement sites were most likely located a little higher up, away from the valley floor.

Two such sites were found through aerial photography only a short distance upslope from the valley locations we have just discussed. Near Ryall's Farm, Gussage, a large enclosure (*see* **71**) with a ditch almost 2m deep, produced pottery spanning the late Bronze to early Iron Ages. A very similar sequence was revealed in the enclosure ditch at Monkton Up Wimborne (*see* MUW 96 on **50**). These sites are probably just two of a number of settlement foci exploiting these important valley areas.

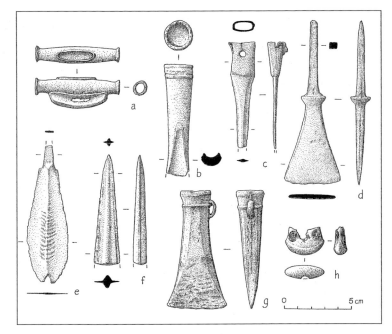

79 Later Bronze Age bronze artefacts from the Gussage valley. 'Bugle' shaped object a, socketed gouge b, socketed knife c, tanged chisel d, razor e, tip of spearhead f, socketed axe g and decorated chape from a scabbard h

A large ring ditch lies about 100m to the east of the Ryall's Farm enclosure and is likely to be the contemporary cemetery for this site. When we look in detail at the ring ditches on the east side of the Gussage valley a very clear pattern emerges (*see* **78**). The local topography reveals a series of short dry valleys, about a kilometre apart, descending south-west from the ridge on Gussage Down to the valley floor. Between these valleys are a matching series of ridges and it is on their south-easterly facing slopes that we find the cemeteries. Either consisting of a single mound/ring ditch or a small group, the spacing is remarkably consistent at intervals of about three-quarters of a kilometre. Although at present we only know of the one settlement in this area, at Ryall's Farm, it is very likely each of these small side valleys conceal further settlements to go with the known distribution of burial sites. It is to these cemeteries we shall now turn.

Cemeteries

Later Bronze Age cemeteries are becoming increasingly well known from recent excavations. On Cranborne Chase three have been excavated during the last twenty years to add to those previously known through the excavations of Pitt Rivers and Clay (1927). These cemeteries can take a number of different forms including the erection of a mound or mounds and often involve careful spatial organisation. The Barrow Pleck cemetery (*see* **72**) is a group of mounds shown by Pitt Rivers to be broadly contemporary with the nearby South Lodge enclosure. Four of the mounds contained primary unurned cremations; close to one in barrow 4 the largest in the group, was the base of a Barrel Urn. Barrow 3 contained two primary cremations one with sherds and a group of six secondary cremations in the south-eastern edge of the mound. The mound ditch had a causeway at this point, in the centre of which was another cremation and an adult crouched inhumation had been placed in the eastern causeway terminal. Re-examination by John

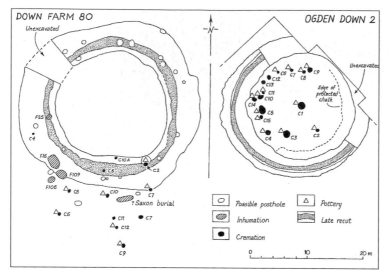

80 Middle Bronze Age cemeteries at Down Farm and Ogden Down

Barrett and Richard Bradley revealed another cremation in the western causeway terminal and six further cremations immediately outside the causeway. In the small barrow 2, Pitt Rivers had found a primary cremation but had failed to locate the surrounding ditch which when recently excavated was also found to have a southerly-facing causeway. Both ditch terminals contained a cremation, one accompanied by the tip of a bronze spear. Barrow 21 contained two primary cremations and 18 produced no burials although during re-excavation a small Victorian urn was uncovered containing, amongst other things, the General's medallion (*see* **19**).

The reuse of earlier mounds for single or groups of burials is well attested in the area. At Down Farm the much remodelled ring ditch **(80),** which lies only 150m to the south-west of the settlement previously discussed, becomes the sites cemetery. Surviving burials here consisted of eleven cremations, two placed in the silted up ditch and the remainder outside to the south. Additionally, a group of three tightly crouched inhumations **(81)** was placed in the same general area just overlapping the ditch. Such a posture would suggest the individuals were bound up shortly after death and may have been wrapped in textiles, reminiscent of 'mummy bundles' found in other cultures.

The grave group consisted of a man, woman and a child accompanied by two shell beads. At the centre of this group was a posthole, perhaps representing a grave marker, and it is tempting to regard them as a family. Why certain individuals were buried in this manner when the bulk of burials recorded at this time were cremations is a matter for speculation. Perhaps they were of different status.

On Handley Hill, Pitt Rivers uncovered an extensive cemetery of 52 separate deposits lying principally to the west and south of barrow 24. The mound itself was probably earlier in date although pits found near the centre were empty.

Other excavated later Bronze Age mounds are known from Bowerchalke and Gussage St.Michael, including barrow 39 at Ogden Down (*see* **80**) which proved to be a two-phased cemetery. In the latter a primary pit yielded a cremation in a small Bucket Urn above which was a further scattered cremation with sherds of another urn and two pieces

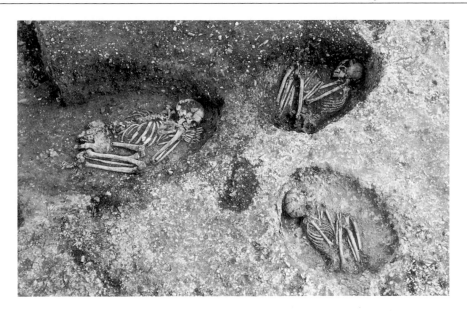

81 Middle Bronze Age burial group uncovered at the Down Farm ring ditch. The group comprised a man left, woman right and a child of about 11 — perhaps a family

of twisted bronze wire, which may once have been parts of a finger ring. The shadow of the mound that survived clearly showed it had at one stage stopped about a metre short of the ditch. In this area on the northern and western sides a series of 14 further cremations had been placed. Three were in Bucket Urns, nine with token sherds and the remainder unaccompanied. The ditch had clearly been recut and deepened by a further 25cm in order to procure enough chalk to cover these additional burials and to possibly re-whiten the mounds. However, this mound was only one component of a remarkable ceremonial complex.

The Ogden Down complex lies close to the south-west end of the Cursus where fieldwork initially revealed three ring ditches and a slightly sunken feature resembling a pond barrow. The sunken feature was soon revealed as a natural eroded patch of clay with flints but during its removal a double row of postholes some 3.25m apart were found to be cut through it. Further excavations traced this avenue to the most northerly of the ring ditches where it was integrated into a double post circle, concentric to the outer edge of the ditch. The inner ring consisted of 18 larger but shallower postholes and the outer 34 smaller but deeper postholes identical in character to the avenue posts (**83**).

Work on the southern end revealed the avenue ended at another, hitherto unsuspected, ring ditch completing a length of 65m (**82, colour plate 19**). The avenue postholes became progressively shallower towards the southern ring ditch with the western line ending some 7m short. As the eastern line continued to the ring ditch it is most likely that three or four postholes of the western line have been ploughed away. Further trenches to the south proved the avenue did not extend further in that direction. Both ring ditches predate the timber elements of the site by well over a millennium with

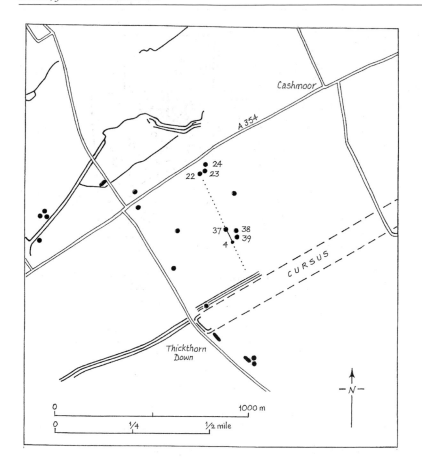

*82 The Ogden Down Ceremonial complex. The axis of the timber avenue had been laid-out from the Cursus and linked ring ditches 4 and 37. Compare with **19***

the northern, partly-recut ring ditch producing two dates: 4010±55BP for the primary ditch and 2810±70BP for the recut. This recut date ties in very well with a date for the inner post circle of 2870±50BP. The southern ring ditch provided nothing to radiocarbon date but did produce a chisel arrowhead from near the ditch base suggesting a construction date also in the third millennium BC. A single severely plough damaged cremation in the very base of an urn of Middle Bronze Age date towards the east side of the mound was the only surviving internal feature. A further unexcavated ring ditch 38 lay between 39 and 37 and just to the west of the avenue, close to the clay-with-flints patch, were traces of possible domestic activity. Here two postholes, a scatter of stakeholes and a large shallow 'working' hollow produced a few scraps of later Bronze Age pottery and flintwork suggesting a domestic focus may lie just beyond the excavated area.

The remains uncovered at Ogden Down brought to light a group of monuments that were linked both physically and by association. In the later Neolithic at least two mounds (4 and 37) were built on a NNW/SSE axis perpendicular to the Cursus which lay 300m to the south. Projecting this alignment 300m to the north, a further group of plough-damaged mounds are reached. Although undated by excavation I recovered the remains of three plough-damaged Middle Bronze Age cremations from mound 23 in 1970. It is possible that one if not all of these mounds has a Neolithic origin, which if so, would

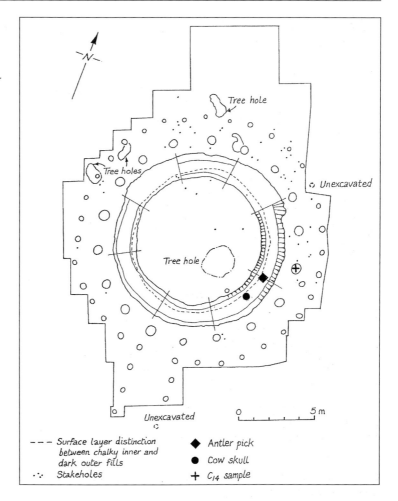

83 Detailed plan of Ogden Down 3 with its surrounding timber circles integrated into the avenue at the southern end

stretch the original alignment to 600m with mound 37 at the centre. Towards the end of the second millennium BC the axis is dramatically reinforced by the building of the timber avenue between mounds 4 and 37 and the timber circles surrounding 37. Further embellishment includes the construction and subsequent remodelling of the cemetery barrow 39, the insertion of at least one cremation in mound 4, the recutting of the ditch of 37 and probably the construction of mound 38. To the north we have the three undated mounds 22, 23, and 24. Here a similar constructional sequence can be postulated. As mound 22 shares the axis it is likely to have a Neolithic origin with 23, which has produced Middle Bronze Age burials, and 24, both likely to be later embellishments.

The timber elements at this site are both exceptionally rare and late in the sequence of timber circle construction within Britain. In Gibson's (1998) comprehensive account of timber circles, Ogden Down appears as the latest reliably dated timber circle in Britain although the tradition continued much longer in Ireland. Only the site of Standlake 20 in Oxfordshire is immediately comparable. It consists of a ring ditch with an external post circle similar to the inner ring at Ogden and produced pottery of later Bronze Age date. Combinations of timber circles and avenues are very few and include the Durrington

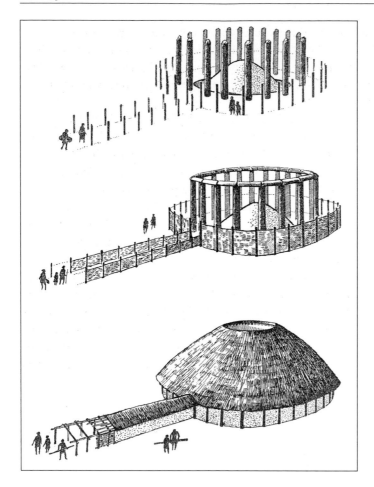

*84 Alternative interpretations of the timber structures revealed at Ogden Down. Compare with **20** (D. Bennett)*

north circle and Stonehenge 1, both of much earlier date. The only site of comparable date is the site of Barrow 1 Poole also in Dorset (Case 1952). Here a ring of posts 8.5m in diameter lay inside a penannular ring ditch. Six postholes located on the causeway appeared to form a flared entrance to the monument. Leading from this for a distance of 4.5m was an unevenly spaced double row of posts, three each side forming an unconvincing avenue some 70cm wide which nevertheless provides the best parallel for Ogden Down.

How do we reconstruct the timber elements revealed at this site? We are never likely to know its true original appearance so all we can do is provide a number of possible options. **84** and **colour plate 20** provide a few of these, from the minimalist approach of simple free-standing posts, to the maximum option of roofed enclosure. My personal feeling is that we may well be dealing with a site nearer the maximum end of the spectrum. The width of the outer post circle of 17m is within the size range of houses of the succeeding Iron Age and the care taken in pairing the avenue posts suggests they may have been bridged.

Either way, the evidence we have here seems to suggest a journey by the living for the dead along the avenue to the enclosed barrow where human remains were probably once deposited. The added impact of roofed enclosure is easy to imagine with a journey along a dark passage until a white mound of chalk, perhaps gleamingly illuminated by torches, is reached. Separated from the mound by the encircling ditch, participants may have progressed around it between the two circles of posts, perhaps witnessing rites undertaken by priests on the mound itself.

Later Bronze Age cemeteries, although exhibiting a wide variety of form and spatial organisation, also show certain similarities. The treatment of the dead is invariably cremation, although an increasing number of tightly crouched burials are now being recognised. The burial area not only includes the mound but often spreads into the ditch and beyond, particularly to the south and south-east. Primary Late Bronze Age mounds often have a causeway through the ditch in this area too. We have already seen that roundhouses invariably have their entrances aligned to the south-east and south-easterly facing slopes are often chosen locations for cemeteries. It would seem that orientation towards the rising sun was as important for the dead as it was for the living.

Cremations are either unaccompanied within an urn, or with a few token sherds with little evidence for social distinction. The urns, identical in form to the pots found within the settlements, are often old, damaged or repaired before they became receptacles for the dead, suggesting that they had seen earlier, heavy domestic use. Grave goods are rare and it seems that much greater emphasis is placed on the ownership of land rather than in the high status goods we saw in the earlier part of the period, a trend that continues in the succeeding Iron Age.

8 A full and well-tended land:
the achievement of Iron Age farmers

The remaining seven centuries before the Roman conquest witnessed the full development of the agronomic potential of the landscape. Field systems became widespread while other areas, possibly reserved for stock rearing, were defined by elaborate earthworks. Towards the middle of the period settlements are commonplace with hillforts on the periphery. This highly efficient management undoubtedly led to a surplus of agricultural production that was stored within the hillforts. This enabled those living within to gain power and status through the control of these commodities. Gradually a number of these sites rose to prominence and dominated larger areas at the expense of others, which were then subsequently abandoned. As a result loose confederations of neighbouring groups eventually led to the formation of tribal units. The recovery of stylistically similar pottery from the settlements and hillforts shows that Cranborne Chase occupied the north-eastern corner of a tribal territory inhabited by the Durotriges **(85)**. By the first century BC the Durotriges were involved in considerable cross channel trade, a lot of which was conducted through the port of Hengistbury Head (Cunliffe 1987). Ready access to the port from the interior was provided by the south-easterly flowing streams which dissect the area. These meet the major rivers of the Avon and Stour on the edge of the area and are eventually discharged into Christchurch harbour close to Hengistbury.

Political pressures resulting from Caesar's campaigns in Gaul in the mid-first-century BC saw the gradual demise of cross channel trade from Hengistbury and the rise of new trading centres in eastern England, controlled by tribes sympathetic to Rome. The fiercely anti-Roman stance adopted by the Durotriges led to the area becoming an economic backwater in the last century before the conquest.

Hillforts

A dozen hillforts are known in the area **(85),** most of them close to the periphery and occupying ridge positions overlooking the major river valley boundaries. The Stour corridor on the south-west perimeter is dominated by the huge forts of Hod and Hambledon **(colour plate 2),** where it enters the area, and Badbury Rings to the south, where it leaves. The Avon valley too has the hillforts of Clearbury and Whitsbury close to its western edge, emphasising the importance of these communication arteries.

From evidence elsewhere in Wessex we know hillforts evolve from simple single rampart and ditch (univallate) constructions to multivallate forms with elaborate entrances built towards the end of the period. A large number of the early forts appear to be abandoned whilst a few become enlarged and elaborated such as Hambledon. Here survey suggests the initial fort enclosed an area of 4.85ha (12 acres) at the northern end of the hill but was extended later, possibly in two phases, to enclose a final area of some 12.5ha (31 acres). Aerial photography reveals the sloping interior to be crowded with house sites.

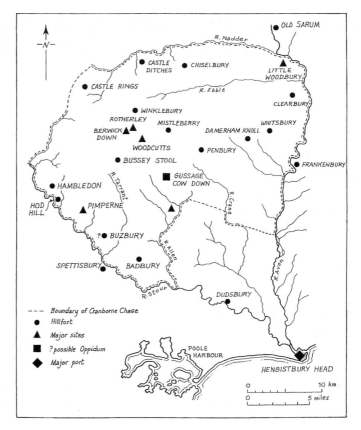

85 Cranborne Chase hill-forts and other important Iron Age sites mentioned in the text

Very occasionally, as at Winkelbury Hill **(colour plate 22)** on the northern escarpment, hillforts are reduced in size. The early excavations of Pitt Rivers (1888) elucidated a three-phase sequence. Initially, the dramatic spur of downland was cut off from the south by two massive straight stretches of bank and ditch, set askew one another to provide a large entrance gap. The discovery of artefacts, including part of a shale ring on the old ground surface beneath this rampart, suggests that this was predated by an even earlier phase of open settlement. Later an attempt to enclose the whole spur was undertaken by linking a 'U'-shaped earthwork up to the phase I earthworks. This phase never appears to have been fully completed as evidenced by the scattered dumps of rampart material and failure to complete the awkward joins with the phase I earthwork. Finally a much smaller area was enclosed by the addition of a curving ditch which links the northern part of the phase II earthwork forming an almost circular earthwork at the tip of the spur. This phase III earthwork plainly cuts the phase II rampart on the western side. Clearly this final enclosure has more in common with settlements of Little Woodbury type (p121) than with hillforts.

For a more detailed view of hillfort defensive systems we must turn to Hod Hill **(86)**. Excavations here revealed the sequence of defensive development (Richmond 1968). A palisaded enclosure appears to belong to the earliest defensive phase, which was then replaced by a timber-faced rampart and ditch: phase II. Later, when the facing became unstable, replacement uprights were set two metres behind the original line. Subsequent developments saw the abandonment of the timber facing and the cutting back of the ditch and bank. This formed a continuous steep slope from the base of the ditch to the top of the bank, known as a 'glacis' rampart, and the creation of a counter-scarp bank and ditch. These defences enclose an area of some 22ha (55 acres). Access to the fort was through two gateways in the north-east and south-west corners. Finally, in the last Iron Age phase, an attempt at multi-vallation was abandoned prematurely, due presumably to the Roman conquest.

After the conquest in 43AD, a legionary fort was constructed within the north-west corner of the Iron Age fort, the inhabitants of which were no doubt forced to flee. Traces of house platforms and other slight earthworks which survive in the unploughed south-eastern corner suggest a densely occupied interior. The remainder of the interior was ploughed extensively during the nineteenth century, bringing a wealth of artefacts to the surface. These were purchased from the farmhands by an enthusiastic local collector, Henry Durden of Blandford. Not content with these surface finds there is evidence to suggest he actively encouraged the workers to dig for artefacts. He eventually amassed a nationally important collection from the hill (Brailsford 1962) which was fortunately purchased for posterity with other material by the British Museum shortly after his death in 1892.

The need to give a context for this material eventually led the British Museum to mount a series of excavations upon the hill during the 1950s led by Sir Ian Richmond. This was the first excavation ever to be undertaken in this country by the British Museum. These excavations enabled the sequence and structure of the defences, already outlined above, to be constructed as well as providing information on living conditions within the fort by the uncovering of a number of roundhouses. These post-built houses still retained remains of their lower foundations in the form of a mass of collapsed chalk and flint. The collapsed remains helped to preserve the floor deposits, which included carefully laid hearths of flint nodules. Deposits of slingstones were frequently found just inside the entrances, prompting the excavator to suggest 'a bagful ready for the occupier to seize as he left the hut'. Some houses were set within compounds where evidence for domestic activities, pits for storage and accommodation for animals was discovered. One house was set within its own rectilinear ditched enclosure, which alone suggests its special significance. However, further evidence of special status is shown by the course of one of the tracks emanating from the main north-east gate which heads directly to this enclosure. Within the house itself two iron spearheads were found instead of the customary slingstones, and at the time of the Roman conquest it seems to have been singled out for special bombardment as evidenced by the finding of a number of ballista boltheads. Surely, as the excavator suggests, we must be dealing with the residence of the local chieftain.

A much smaller horseshoe-shaped enclosure provided some evidence for the religious and ceremonial side of life within the fort. Inside three pits were found two with burials and the third with votive offerings of a bronze loop fastener and six valuable iron items. The first burial pit produced a contracted skeleton of an adult female with an infant between her knees. They had been provided with an iron bound wooden bucket, latch-

86 Aerial photograph of Hod Hill from the southwest. The Roman fort can be seen in the left-hand corner

lifter, bobbin, two loomweights and meat in the form of several animal jaws for the next world. This apparently domestic array of artefacts prompted the excavator to state: 'these are the mortal remains of a housewife, buried with her infant child and some household equipment'. At a slightly deeper level in the pit a lower left leg and foot of another individual were found which may possibly have been all that remained of an earlier burial disturbed by the 'housewife's' grave. In the upper levels of the third pit another crouched adult female burial was uncovered. Although devoid of artefacts this time, below her in the lower levels of the pit, another significant group of objects was found. These comprised the bronze fittings from a wooden vessel, part of a shale bracelet and a number of iron items including a spearhead, socket, brooch, spiral ring and knife. It is clear from the valuable nature of these caches of objects that we are dealing with something more than mere rubbish disposal. The enclosure, which is likely to be one of a number within the fort, probably represents a small family shrine where the various rites connected with death and worship of the gods were observed.

In general the picture that emerges from the limited investigations within the developed hillforts of Cranborne Chase is one of dense occupation and thriving communities. Here surplus produce generated by the surrounding farms and settlements was stored and through the control and eventual disposal of these surpluses those living within the hillforts gained their power and status. It is to these farms and settlements, the mainstay of the Iron Age economy, that we shall now turn.

As we have seen, by the end of the Bronze Age a large number of settlement units are defined by some form of partial or wholly enclosing ditch, making them much easier for archaeologists to locate. Although open settlements undoubtedly also existed at this time, the dense distribution of ditched or partly ditched enclosures suggest this is the more normal settlement type. These enclosures can take many forms and vary in size considerably (**87**). Located just within the north-eastern boundary of the Chase is the site of Little Woodbury (Bersu 1940). This ditched enclosure was the focus of a pioneering excavation in the 1930s by the great German archaeologist Gerhard Bersu. Here about half of the 1.6ha (4 acres) enclosure was uncovered revealing a substantial roundhouse in

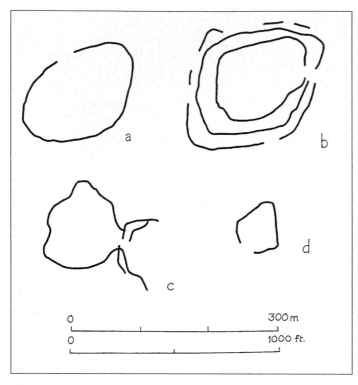

the centre, 13.7m in diameter with its entrance directly in line with the main gate. Nearby was a smaller roundhouse and scattered across the interior were many storage pits, two post 'drying racks' and a series of large irregular shallow pits termed 'working hollows'. These latter features probably began life as small chalk quarries but were later utilised for various processing activities. Towards the back of the enclosure a number of four-post granaries were uncovered which may have been used to store the grain for more immediate use. The settlement, which probably housed an extended family group, became the 'type site' for classifying this common form of economic unit and gave rise to the term 'Little Woodbury Culture'.

A much larger 4.65ha (11.5 acres), though similar enclosure was examined at Pimperne in the early 1960s (Harding et al 1993). Here the remains of a large roundhouse 15m in diameter was uncovered **(88)**, the plan of which was later used for a splendid reconstruction at Butser Hill Experimental Centre **(colour plate 23)**.

A more recent and complete excavation took place on a similar enclosure at Gussage All Saints in 1972 (Wainwright 1979). Here a circular enclosure produced a similar range of evidence to Little Woodbury although less of the actual buildings survived due to heavy ploughing. The site was occupied throughout the period and underwent considerable remodelling during the three main phases identified.

The first phase enclosure ditch only 80cm deep provided material for an external bank and enclosed an area of 1.2ha (3 acres). Four small simple gap entrances were noted on the north and west with the main entrance, a 20m gap, located in the east. This gap was closed by two antenna ditches of more substantial proportions that flared out from a four metre

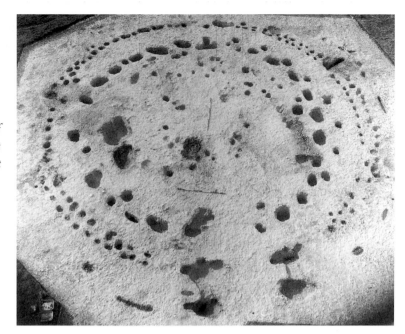

88 *Iron Age roundhouse under excavation at Pimperne in 1961. The multiple rings of postholes present suggested at least two separate phases of construction* (Copyright I.M. Blake and D.W. Harding)

wide causeway. Behind this lay a strong gateway constructed at the southern end of the enclosure ditch. Within the enclosure large numbers of pits (128) and 14 four-post structures were revealed. A fairly consistent layout of these features was observed comprising a wide circular zone of storage pits, set well inside the ditch, which surrounded a group of four-post structures. No house sites had survived the extensive ploughing but it is likely they were located in the broad zone mostly devoid of storage structures behind the enclosure ditch on the north, east and south sides. During phase II the ditch was enlarged and the small gap entrances were infilled. New larger antenna ditches were dug on different alignments, which led from the more substantial replaced gate thus creating a far grander approach to the site. Internal organisation consisted of storage pits arranged in a broad arc inside the northern and western sides of the ditch in areas previously left clear of pits, and traces of two roundhouses at the rear of the enclosure. Interestingly, although the number of pits was about half that of phase I, their size was much greater, allowing for similar storage capacities in both phases.

The final Durotrigean phase which commenced in the first century BC saw the creation of a number of internal subsidiary enclosures. The most dramatic of these is the penannular enclosure appended to the eastern side and cutting away part of the main enclosure ditch in this area. This feature has been dated to the second quarter of the first century AD and is likely to have been built in quick response to some external threat and in order to protect the timber structure(s) within. Only a few postholes of this phase survived inside including the gate but it is likely that a substantial house, perhaps belonging to the headman, lay inside. An apparently similar arrangement has been observed within one of the Gussage Down enclosures **(colour plate 25)**. Further internal arrangements include a trapezoidal enclosure, possibly for stock management, with perhaps a semi-circular annex on its west side. Storage capacity increased substantially during this phase suggesting an increase in population, 46 of whom were found buried in pits and ditches. Only eight burials were recorded from phase I and II contexts but a general scatter of isolated bones found in features indicate excarnation may have been the general method of disposal of the dead at this time.

Surviving evidence for craft industries included bone and antler working, weaving, shale turning and metalworking. Although there was some evidence to show that both iron and bronze were being worked at the site in all three phases, including iron smelting in phase III, it is from the end of phase II that the most spectacular evidence survived.

In the lower levels of a pit close to the entrance of the enclosure a series of tips of casting debris was recovered. The fragile remnants of several hundred clay moulds lay together with fragments of at least 30 crucibles, a bronze billett and four bone modelling tools used for making the wax patterns around which the clay moulds were invested. The remarkably fresh condition of this material indicates a localised area of industrial activity, which was only preserved due to being tipped into the adjacent pit. It was clear from the shape of the moulds that they had produced fittings for chariots and pony harnesses of both simple and elaborate forms. The bulk of these consisted of terrets and strap unions for guiding reins and linking straps respectively, bridle bits, and linch or axel pins for the chariots. It was calculated from the material that survived that at least fifty sets of harness and chariot fittings had been produced in a period of only a year or two. The amount of organisation required in this production suggests that this was not a casual activity undertaken by an itinerant smith but was more likely the work of a number of resident craftsman who were specialists in working wood, leather and metal. It is probable that this workshop provided sets of finished harness and chariots to many of the contemporary settlements known to exist in the immediate area, including an almost identical site only 1km across the valley to the north-east. Indeed surface finds of a terret fragment and bronze dipped iron bridle link, of types known to have been produced at Gussage, have already been recovered from two nearby settlements **(89)**. It is unlikely, however, that many such artefacts have survived intact. The valuable nature of the metal would have ensured that the bulk of items were recycled once they became worn out or damaged.

Although this, at present unique, deposit of metalworking debris is of national importance we must not be tempted into assuming that the site was of particularly high status. It is likely that many such workshops existed serving their local areas. Indeed many excavated settlements of this period yield some evidence of metalworking. Therefore it seems most likely it was just extreme good fortune that preserved the fragile material at Gussage. Produced in just one short phase of activity its rapid burial, before trampling and weathering could so easily have destroyed it, ensured its survival.

Analysis of the animal bones revealed sheep (from 46-60 %) as the dominant domestic species in the three phases. Cattle contributed 20%-28%, and pig 8%-14%. The ages at death show that sheep were used mainly for milk and wool production while cattle provided most of the meat consumed. Horse remains consisted entirely of adults suggesting that no breeding was practised and that more probably periodic round-ups were made of selected animals for training purposes. Domestic poultry included duck, goose and fowl. Both cats and dogs were present and included complete skeletons of very young animals, suggesting deliberate culling. Numerous wild species were represented,

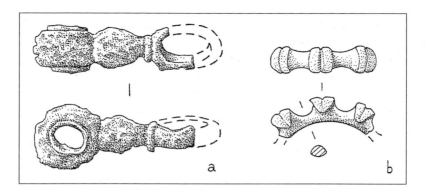

89 Bronze terret fragment b, and bridle link a, of types manufactured at Gussage All Saints and found on nearby contemporary settlements

particularly birds which must have made a useful contribution to the food supply. Remains of buzzards and most unusually hen harrier may represent individuals killed for raiding poultry. Plant remains suggest a gradual transition from barley to wheat and legumes throughout the three phases.

Gussage demonstrates a continuity of occupation throughout the Iron Age and into the latter first century AD. Such a situation contrasts markedly with the sites at Berwick Down near Tollard Royal (Wainwright 1968) where sequential shifting of settlement locations seems to have taken place. The sites here consist of an unenclosed group of pits with at least one substantial roundhouse, a circular enclosure containing many hut platforms and a kite-shaped enclosure to the south. Although unexcavated it is possible to put forward tentative dating for the first two sites. Using the analogy of other sites in Wessex it is clear that an unenclosed group of pits and roundhouse(s) is likely to date to the earlier Iron Age. The enclosed group is believed to be later because of the large amounts of Romano-British pottery that has been turned up in mole hills and rabbit scrapes. The kite-shaped enclosure was completely excavated in 1965, revealing the remains of a Durotrigean farmstead **(90)**, constructed during the century prior to the Roman conquest. The single roundhouse and group of storage facilities found within suggest a comparatively short period of occupation — perhaps a century at most. After the conquest the settlement focus shifted a hundred metres or so to the north.

The nearby settlements of Woodcutts and Rotherley were both shown by the excavations of Pitt Rivers (1887 and 1888) to have begun during the first two centuries BC, but unlike Berwick the two settlements continued to be occupied throughout the Roman period, during which they underwent considerable changes. This pattern of development is true of many of the Chase settlements constructed in the latter part of the period when new forms of occupation sites are appearing including the distinctive 'banjo' enclosures.

Succinctly described by Cunliffe (1993), banjo enclosures are 'usually roughly circular, about a quarter of a hectare in extent, are defined by a ditch which continues out from both sides of the entrance to flank a narrow approach road before opening out, often

90 Reconstruction of the Berwick Down farmstead as it may have appeared in the early first century AD (D. Bennett)

at right angles on either side of the road to join more complex systems of linear ditches'. Occasionally these ditches double back behind the 'banjos' to encompass them within larger enclosures such as those upon Gussage Down. The four or possibly five enclosures of this kind are only a part of the whole settlement complex which must be the largest of its type recorded in Wessex (Corney in Barrett et al 1991).

The originally well-preserved earthworks were first recorded by Colt Hoare, who described them as 'one of the most interesting relics of antiquity which our island can produce'. It was clearly a place which appealed greatly to the learned antiquary as he was later to remark, 'How often have I reviewed with fresh delight this truly interesting ground, which elucidates so strongly the history and manners of the primitive Britons'. Charles Warne re-drew Colt Hoare's plan for his Ancient Dorset in 1872 but had little of value to add to his concise description. He supported Hoare's idea that the site was Vindocladia, as described in the Antonine Itinerary, but this is no longer accepted and most archaeologists today would place it at Shapwick, just south of Badbury Rings. It was not until the 1920s when O.G.S. Crawford and Alexander Keiller published their pioneering book of aerial photographs *Wessex From The Air* that additional detail of the complex was revealed. Despite 'the encroachments of the plough', substantial parts of the main settlement complex still survived after the First World War **(91)**. Their final demise only came during World War II when these venerable tracts of downland were brought under the plough and remain so today.

Aerial photography continues to add important detail to our knowledge of the

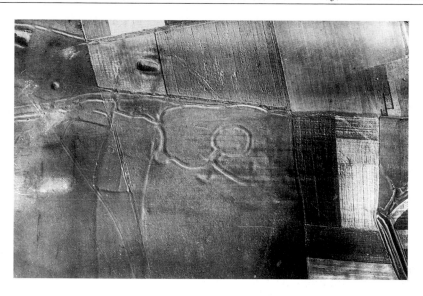

91 Early aerial photograph taken in 1924 by Crawford and Keiller of Gussage Down during their work for 'Wessex from the Air' published in 1928. The Dorset Cursus can be seen crossing from top to bottom towards the left hand side where it incorporates one of the long barrows. A well preserved 'banjo' enclosure is clearly visible in the centre but sadly it did not survive the later depredations of wartime ploughing measures. (By permission of English Heritage copyright reserved)

92 Detailed plan of the great complex of earthworks on Gussage Down. After Bowen 1990 with additions (By permission of English Heritage copyright reserved)

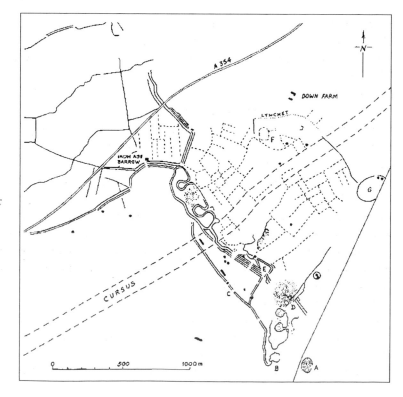

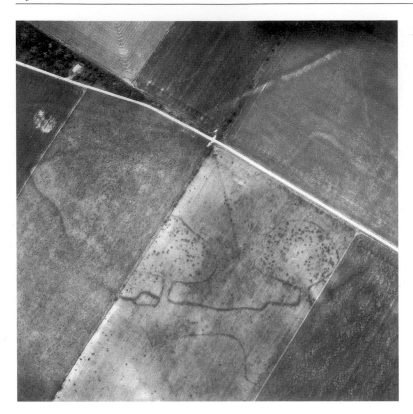

93 The southerly double 'banjo' enclosure complex on Gussage Down was first revealed by this remarkable photograph taken by John Boyden in 1978. (By permission of English Heritage copyright reserved)

complex and this has allowed the Royal Commission to produce updated plans in 1975 and in 1990. Using the latest plan, with additions **(92),** as our guide I shall describe the complex from the south-east across the downland to the north western perimeter — a distance of more than 2km.

At point A, an oval enclosure probably of 'banjo' type has part of its entrance overlain by the Ackling Dyke. Opposite this at B, an irregular enclosure appears to be the starting point for C, a ditch that defines the western edge of the complex. Immediately to the north of B is the first linked pair of banjo enclosures **(93)**. Visible within are large numbers of pits clearly showing the enclosures were occupied. To the north of these features is an area strewn with occupation debris of late Iron Age and Roman date. Within it are two rectilinear enclosures and at D a spread of building debris can be defined, including painted wall plaster of a Roman building. Large numbers of coins and a miniature bronze spearhead found in this area suggest it may have been the site of a Romano-Celtic temple. A double ditched track heads south-west from this location whilst another ditch heading north-east may define the limits of this part of the complex. At point E are various lengths of multiple ditches that appear to overlie an earlier rectilinear enclosure. To the north of this is a further enclosure, only partly revealed by aerial photography, with clear evidence of occupation and internal structures **(colour plate 25)**. Multiple ditches then link to the northern pair of banjos. Between them a major spread of occupation debris continues as far as the limits of the northern enclosure but not beyond it. Forming the northern boundary is a system of multiple ditches. Lying just

94 Iron Age bronze small finds from Cranborne Chase. La Tène I brooches a and b, toggle c, awl d, decorative mount e, ring-headed pin f, stud with inset engraved silver sheet g, and La Tène III brooch h

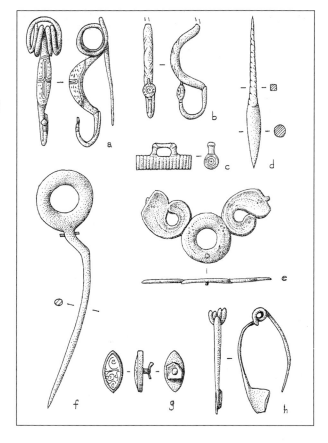

outside these a barrow excavated in 1969 (White 1970) yielded the remains of a primary late Iron Age cremation.

Just south of Down Farm a major lynchet follows the change in soil types. This forms the northern boundary of the complex as far as the Drive Plantation enclosure, G, where evidence of both bronze and iron working has been recovered. Nestling behind the western edge of this lynchet lies an enclosure at point F. Here minor excavations (Green 1985) have revealed traces of an embanked Early Iron Age settlement with only a short stretch of ditch on its western side. The portion of the Cursus enclosed by the complex appears to have influenced the development of the field systems in this area, which seem to represent the main arable block serving the community. To the south-west of the down no evidence of field systems is found but linear earthworks partly define a large area some 700ha (1730 acres) in extent which may have been used for stock management.

It appears significant that in an area where Mid-Late Iron Age settlements are thick on the ground this major block of land is apparently devoid of them. However, the meadows to the north of the present village of Gussage St Michael have produced, particularly on the eastern side, a number of small finds **(94)** but little contemporary pottery to suggest occupation. Moreover, it seems likely that the stream here was an important focus for daily activities, particularly for the watering of stock belonging to settlements located outside this immediate area. Elsewhere on the Chase, at least nine other settlement

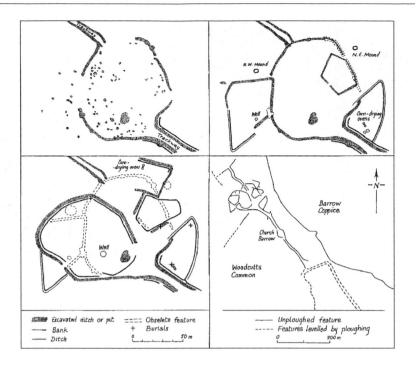

95 The main phases of the Woodcutts Iron Age — Romano-British settlement. Phase I consists of a 'banjo' enclosure begun in the late Iron Age (top left). In Phase II a number of ancillary enclosures are constructed from the late second century AD (top right). Phase III, begun in the early fourth century AD, sees the extensive destruction of the original Iron Age enclosure and its replacement with a substantially new oval enclosure (bottom left). After RCHME 1975 (By permission of English Heritage copyright reserved)

complexes are known to be based on single banjo enclosures. One was eventually teased out of Pitt Rivers' excavations at the site of Woodcutts (Hawkes 1947) **(95, colour plate 24)**. Careful re-examination of the General's records revealed a first phase Iron Age enclosure that was subsequently added to after the Roman invasion. Finds from the Cranborne Chase enclosures argue for construction during the first and second century BC. Numerous storage pits visible inside suggests that they were occupied, and the frequent finds of Durotrigan coins would imply that occupation was of reasonably high status. Further finds of sherds of pre-conquest amphorae support this idea and it has been suggested that Cranborne Chase may have been a separate sub-Durotrigean territory with Gussage Down as its main centre. The combination of multiple defensive ditch systems defining large settlement areas, high status finds and the lack of a developed hillfort in the heart of the area has promoted the idea of Gussage Down being an oppidum (Corney in Barrett et al 1991).

Certainly, when we piece together all the information currently available, a picture emerges of a well-populated and carefully organised landscape **(96)**. The efficient farming practice no doubt produced a surplus wealth enabling trade to develop and thereby further

96 Aerial photograph of the Iron Age enclosed settlement on Oakley Down (top right) and part of its contemporary field system. The latter is partly aligned on earlier burial monuments

enhancing the status of those who controlled the surpluses. Local leaders would have been able to display their wealth by conspicuous consumption and use of objects as well as by exchange, and in so doing would help cement relationships and alliances with neighbours. Skilled craftsmen were evidently employed to produce fine fittings for horses and chariots — the most mobile demonstration of wealth and power a community could display. Perhaps with the demise of Hengistbury as a cross-channel port in the century before the conquest, the area may have become gradually isolated, helping to produce a fiercely anti-Roman stance. At least 20 'oppida' (major settlements) were conquered during the invasion, many of which would have lain in Durotrigean territory. It should come as no surprise that the need to subjugate this large and volatile population manifested itself in the construction of one of the most impressive Roman road 'aggers' (raised causeways) in the country, Ackling Dyke, and the unique instance of a legionary fort built within the native fort at Hod Hill. The building of the Ackling Dyke also caused the destruction of a number of settlements along its path, a further reminder of the formidable might of Rome.

9 Continuity to abandonment and renewal:
historical developments from Romano-British to Medieval times

During the Roman invasion period of AD43/44 the Durotrigean tribal area put up fierce resistance. The commander of the invading army, Vespasian, was known to have conquered over 20 oppida on his westward campaign. Although well defended, the occupiers were unable to cope with the technological might of well-drilled troops wielding advanced military hardware. Remarkable evidence of such hardware comes from two Dorest hillforts, where use of the ballista has been demonstrated. This weapon, a sort of gigantic crossbow, was capable of accurately showering bundles of arrows over considerable distances. The largest house platform within Hod Hill, presumably belonging to the chieftain, was found to have a scattering of over 20 of these bolt heads, suggesting repeated bombardment. Even more dramatic was the discovery of a number of burials within a native cemetery at the great hillfort of Maiden Castle in the south of the county. Here a few individuals had sustained injuries inflicted by the ballista including one individual who still had a bolt head embedded in his spine. Ballista heads and small pieces of Roman military equipment have occasionally been found on minor settlements within the area, suggesting a thorough subjugation of the large native population. Shortly afterwards, military forts suddenly appear both at Lake Farm near Wimborne and within the ramparts of Hod Hill, the latter sufficient to hold a legionary detachment of some 600 men plus an auxiliary cavalry unit of 250 (no doubt capable of quelling any local revolt) (*see* **86**).

Within a few years of these events the Roman road system would have been under construction and Badbury Rings, a former Iron Age hillfort, became a focal point for the distribution of the local network. Traversing the area westwards was the road to Bath and to the north lay the impressive Ackling Dyke, part of the great west road from London to Exeter, via Old Sarum (Soriodunum). The agger of this road is remarkably high in places bearing in mind it crosses a well-drained area of downland. It was probably built on this scale to impress the large local populace and to keep them quietly occupied as they were no doubt coerced into building it. On Oakley Down some of the metalling is clearly visible and reveals a makeup of sands and pebbles from Reading bed deposits. The nearest source of such material is on Pentridge Hill about 2km away, and ancient quarry workings still present may have been connected with this episode of road building. Following the road's course south over Gussage Down it can be shown to cut deliberately through two native settlement enclosures, another reminder of the dominance of Rome to any would-be insurgents.

*97 Distribution of Romano-
British sites in the study area*

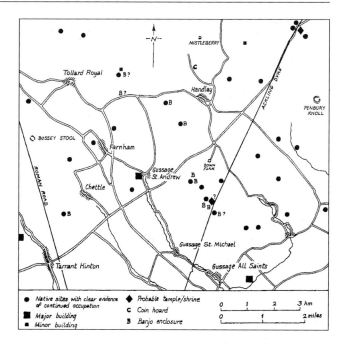

After the initial invasion period, life would have settled back down to something approaching normality for the local native population. Many of the settlements were still in use and from coin evidence alone they appear to have continued well into the latter half of the fourth century **(97)**. The maintenance of the agricultural regime would have been an advantage to the Roman administration who had no wish to abandon a system that had been consistently productive prior to the invasion. However, it is clear that the bulk of these surpluses were no longer converted into luxuries as in the later Iron Age but were sent instead to swell the Imperial coffers through taxation.

The appearance of more substantial houses built of mortared flint walls, plastered internally and roofed with limestone or clay roof tiles, reveal that a few families were gradually able to accrue wealth. Traces of just such a building were found by Pitt Rivers at Woodcutts where the inhabitants were furnished with the luxury of on the spot water provided by two wells, one 57m deep.

By the third and fourth centuries a few families even became sufficiently wealthy to be able to construct impressive villas locally **(98)**. Here, as elsewhere in Wessex, recent excavations have invariably shown that they were built over earlier pre-Roman settlements. It seems apparent, as Cunliffe has recently stated that: 'not only were many of the farming units of the pre-conquest period maintained well into the Roman era, an observation which argues forcefully for a continuity of land ownership, but also the families who inherited them were able to acquire sufficient wealth to invest in providing increasingly comfortable accommodation which, in a few cases could verge on the luxurious'.

Just such a luxurious establishment was built at Rockbourne that comprised over 70 rooms, a few provided with mosaics and underfloor heating set around a courtyard. This was undoubtedly the administrative centre for a large estate whose lands may have

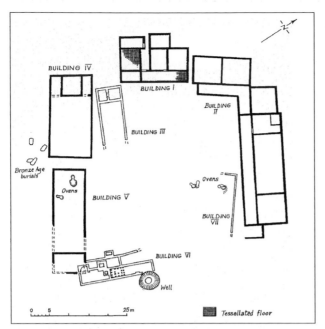

98 Barton Hill Roman villa, Tarrant Hinton. After Giles 1981 (Dorset Natural History and Archaeological Society)

extended as far north and west as the large stock compounds found on Rockbourne Down and Soldier's Ring, near Damerham. Minor excavations at the former site undertaken by Heywood Sumner (1914) also revealed much evidence for grain processing including several 'T'-shaped driers.

Further substantial building complexes include the villa at Tarrant Hinton (Giles 1981), Pitt Rivers' last excavation at Iwerne Minster (Hawkes 1947), and from the author's own fieldwork at Knowlton and Minchington. Interestingly both Tarrant Hinton and Minchington had featured in earlier antiquarian accounts. The former was noted by the Blandford antiquary William Shipp, who recorded in his diary a visit to the field in which it lay in 1845 (Dorset County Museum, *Shipp Diaries Vol III* 1862). He had been drawn to the spot by the farmer who complained that his 'crops observed to wither on the occurrence of the last drought'. A very early record for crop marks! Shipp undertook some digging on the site and uncovered portions of tessellated pavements including one he recorded in an unusual watercolour **(99)**. The site was then forgotten until major excavations 1968-84 revealed the complete ground plan of a courtyard villa **(98)**.

Shipp also noted the discovery of Roman buildings near Minchington in 1868 in a field called Oak Hill. Working on updating the 2nd edition of Hutchins' *History of Dorset* at the time, he included the new find in the later work (Hutchins *Vol III* 1868). However, the exact location was vague and no further evidence of Roman buildings in the area was uncovered until my own fieldwork in 1987 revealed a site which fitted the previous account. Although not certainly the site recorded by Shipp it does bear many similarities to his description, even down to details such as dice sized red and white tessarae. The site is now the focus for a long-term project by the local archaeological group (Sparey-Green 1998) and excavations are revealing portions of fine mosaics **(colour plate 26)**. In tandem a nearby, partly contemporary, farming settlement is being investigated by Bournemouth

99 William Shipp's watercolour of the tessellated pavement found at Barton Hill, Tarrant Hinton about 1850. Over a century later excavations uncovered a complete villa (see 98). (Dorset County Museum)

University at Goldfields Farm **(100)**. This is likely to have been part of the estate run by the owners of the villa.

Nevertheless, the bulk of the population continued to live in the downland settlements already established in the Iron Age. It appears from surface evidence that many of the containing enclosures were then neglected and in some cases 'slighted' allowing settlement to spread well beyond the limits originally demarcated by these enclosures. For instance, both banjo complexes on Gussage Down reveal major spreads of Romano-British material well beyond the enclosures themselves. In the northern complex the northernmost enclosure appears to have been deliberately levelled which explains why it does not appear on Colt Hoare's very accurate plan and was not discovered until the advent of aerial photography. A large settlement area grew out from this enclosure, nearly as far as the southerly banjo that appears to have lain just outside this area of settlement. The southern complex reveals a similar pattern with a settlement spreading over and beyond the northern banjo, but not as far south as the southern one. Within this complex settlement area two trapezoidal enclosures are known together with a building of higher status, as revealed by the finding of painted wall plaster and large amounts of fragmentary clay and stone tiles. It may be a small villa although its proximity to the enclosures suggests we are more likely to be dealing with a Romano-Celtic temple complex. A recent find of a miniature votive spearhead (Corney & Green 1987) seems to lend weight to this argument. It is also interesting to note that a clear road is visible on aerial photographs connecting this site to the Ackling Dyke some 300m away, along which

100   *Excavations by Bournemouth University at the Iron Age and Romano-British site on Goldfields Farm near Cashmoor revealed a number of its former inhabitants!*

pilgrims could have progressed to the shrine on the hill.

The Drive Plantation enclosure 1km to the north (*see* **92,** point **G),** however, reveals a different pattern. After being cut by the Ackling Dyke it seems to have been largely abandoned with only a small area on the south side revealing Romano-British occupation. Here traces of a building or buildings with major quantities of iron ore were discovered amongst the rubble, suggesting the likely existence of a wayside smithy. Occasionally settlement sites may have been relocated as in the case of Berwick Down, Tollard Royal. The Durotrigan farmstead we have already discussed appears to have been replaced by a new settlement only 100m away.

Larger market settlements developed alongside the Ackling Dyke at Woodyates and around the road junctions at Badbury Rings. Here, just to the south at Shapwick, a major settlement associated with an enclosure has recently been revealed during extensive geophysical survey by the National Trust (Papworth 1994). Covering a considerable area it can justifiably be regarded as a small town and probably equates to the site of Vindocladia mentioned in the Antonine Itinerary. It is certainly a much better candidate than Gussage Down or Woodyates suggested by Colt Hoare and Pitt Rivers respectively. At this latter site, just to the north of Bokerley Dyke, Pitt Rivers uncovered a number of rectilinear enclosures in the ditches of which were a number of burials. Within one lay a small square earthwork some 38m in diameter containing five graves. Piggott (1974), in his classic work on the Druids, compares the complex to others known on the continent and suggests the area is a Romano-Celtic sanctuary. Large quantities of coins and a number of votive objects found in the general area do indeed suggest that a shrine or temple lies close by.

The relatively peaceful and stable co-existence of these Romano-British communities, which continued for well over three hundred years, seem to have been sharply interrupted by political events in the latter fourth century. Rome's eastern frontier was frequently under barbarian attack and as a consequence large numbers of troops were withdrawn from Britain to fight. This left Britain vulnerable to attack from Picts, Scots and the Germanic tribes to the east. Some of the remaining troops evidently became disaffected and proclaimed their Generals emperors of the Northern Empire in direct defiance of Rome. These revolts were a constant drain on the Empire's resources and Britain was increasingly left to organise its own defence using local militias. Finds of military fittings of this period **(101)** in our area testify to increased defensive activities. It was during this period of unrest that the Bokerley line was recreated with the digging of a massive ditch and bank over 10km long **(colour plate 28).** The effect was to block the Ackling Dyke which helped to protect Dorset from the Saxon advance until the middle of the sixth century. The gradual breakdown of centralised authority coincided with the demise of a market economy and a growing reliance on local barter. Coinage starts to become less common after the reign of Valens (364-378), and practically disappears by the end of the century. Wider lines of communications are severed and increasing isolation is reflected in the paucity of material remains. Although it is probable that the settlements described earlier continued to be occupied, the lack of datable material from recent excavations of these sites makes recognition of activity during the fifth and sixth centuries very difficult.

Saxon evidence

Evidence from cemeteries excavated in the Salisbury area suggests there was a wealthy enclave of Saxons living there at least by the middle of the fifth century. The heartland of Cranborne Chase which lay south of Bokerley Dyke still remained to be conquered and it was not until a century later that the Dyke appears to have been breached and the whole of Dorset brought under Saxon control. During his excavations of the burial mounds on Oakley Down and Woodyates, Colt Hoare revealed a number of intrusive Saxon burials including two rich graves dating to the early period of colonisation. One of these, perhaps significantly sited just behind the Dyke, had been placed within the long barrow that had been enclosed by the sarsen setting we discussed in chapter 4. The extended female burial was furnished with a rich array of grave-goods, including an ivory bracelet, glass beads (one hung with a gold loop), and an exquisite gold and enamelled pendant. Several iron fittings, possibly from a wooden bed or bier, suggest that the burial may have been accompanied by fine textiles. Colt Hoare's barrow 1 at Oakley Down produced a similar extended female secondary burial placed in the top of the mound. She too was provided with fine jewellery including many glass and amber beads and a small gilt face brooch. A further large mound crests the ridge to the south of Oakley Down and overlooks the upper reaches of the Allen Valley at Down Farm. Although Cunnington found no Saxon burials during his examination of this mound, he did find two intrusive extended burials in the easterly of its two smaller attendants. The large mound is mentioned in a Saxon

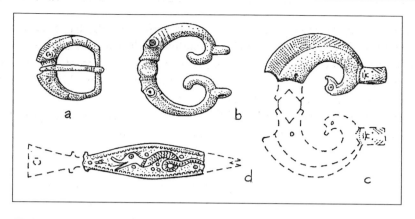

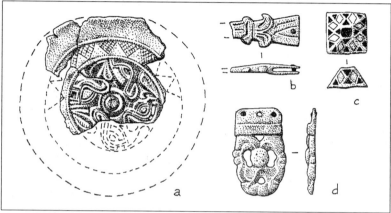

101 Belt buckles and strap-end of fourth-century date from sites on the Chase. Originally thought to be items of exclusively military equipment it is now thought that such pieces of insignia were worn by civil officials about their duties of administration, control and taxation

102 Saxon bronze small finds from the Chase. Sixth-century Style 1 disc brooch a, fifth-/sixth-century strap-end b, seventh-century pyramidal mount from a sword belt c, and a tenth-/eleventh-century strap-end d

land charter as Berendes Beorh and lies at the junction of three parish boundaries. The name Berende means fruitful or productive and probably relates to the great size of the mound. Wor Barrow (chapter 4) is also mentioned in the same charter as Pegan Beorh, or Pega's Brow, a personal name. During his excavations there Pitt Rivers found 17 secondary burials cut into the mound and upper ditch fill. One was undoubtedly associated with a fourth-century coin but the others, several of which were headless and one clearly decapitated, could well be Saxon in date. One wonders whether the mound had become a site of execution.

However, the most spectacular Saxon burial found in Cranborne Chase was that found on the edge of the northern escarpment on Swallowcliffe Down. Excavation of the mound in 1966 (Speake 1989) revealed a partly robbed grave of a young woman dating to the seventh century. Surviving iron and bronze fittings show she had been placed on a wooden bed together with many articles, including both iron and bronze bound yew wood buckets, a maplewood casket, iron pan, bronze censer, leather satchel, and two glass beakers. Her fine jewellery, however, had been removed during the earlier, probably nineteenth century, excavation. Such burials, positioned in fairly isolated but prominent mounds, seem to represent the graves of the local élite who appear to be placed at some distance away from the cemeteries of the bulk of the population.

On Winkelbury Down, not far from the hillfort (chapter 8) a small cemetery of much lower status was uncovered (Pitt Rivers 1898). Once again a group of earlier Bronze Age mounds became the focus for a cemetery with two of the mounds being the recipients of intrusive burials. One of these, unfortunately previously robbed, was placed in a large rectangular pit with postholes in each corner; traces of wood and iron fittings suggest this burial chamber may have been roofed. The remaining 30 graves, grouped in three clusters to the east of the mounds, were clearly of much lower status containing few finds between them. It would seem likely that this cemetery represents part of a small farming community, perhaps grouped around a former leader or elder.

New farms and settlements would have been created in the river valleys where a wider range of resources was available. By this stage the thin downland soils were likely to have suffered exhaustion, and much was probably left to return to pasture whilst the valley sides provided opportunities for intense cultivation. Not surprisingly, evidence for these settlements is sparse, especially when one considers that the bulk of these areas today are either pasture or occupied by villages. Dorset appears to have remained aceramic after the breakdown of the Romano-British pottery industry until the tenth or eleventh century. Even when valley areas are ploughed the absence of the humble potsherd leaves recognition of Saxon activities largely dependent on the much rarer finds of datable metalwork **(102, colour plate 27)**. However, where fieldwork has been sufficiently intense, as in the upper reaches of the Gussage valley, a few such finds hint at settlement from the later sixth century **(104)**.

Interestingly, controlled metal detecting can play an important role in helping understand land use in Saxon and Medieval times by the plotting of small finds. Work of this kind in the parish of Gussage St Michael has revealed likely settlement areas in the valley floor. Some areas were undoubtedly used intensively and yield a great density of finds including small dress fittings such as buckles, strap-ends, chapes and mounts. These areas were clearly well used during Medieval times but undoubtedly started earlier as evidenced by the small but significant number of Saxon finds. Others produce very few, if any, finds and almost certainly represent areas of marginal use like summer grazing.

In his book on Dorset, Christopher Taylor (1970) suggests that a long hedge line bisecting the Gussage valley marks a boundary between two neighbouring estates which may have been created at this time or a little later **(104)**. The northern end of this boundary bisects Down Farm and is perpetuated by the footpath and present farm lane. Many of these estate borders formed the basis of the parish boundaries and system of land division which we are all familiar with today.

Subsequent change within this system often consists of subdivision. The valley settlements, often the precursors of present day villages, developed land units in the form

103   Exceptional ninth-century silver strap-end depicting a helmeted man pruning vines. Found on Cranborne Chase (private possession)

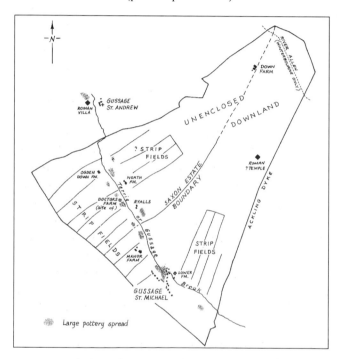

104   Later Saxon and Medieval evidence in the upper Gussage valley

of long narrow strips that dissected the valleys. These provided a range of soil types within each strip, allowing for different land use ranging from the cultivation of root crops in the valley bottoms to hay cutting on the higher chalk slopes. Beyond the strips was probably an area of open down reserved for communal grazing. The remains of just such a system can still clearly be seen in the Gussage valley north of the present village of Gussage St Michael and has been supported by the evidence from metal detecting. The outline of the field systems, which had fully evolved by Medieval times, can be seen in the parallel hedgerows. Some idea of the pattern of occupation has also been revealed by intense fieldwork in the present day arable areas of the valley bottom **(104)**.

Depopulation of the countryside, particularly as a result of the Black Death, caused the abandonment of large numbers of farms and settlements during the Middle Ages. On Cranborne Chase various earthwork remains survive to show us exactly where some of

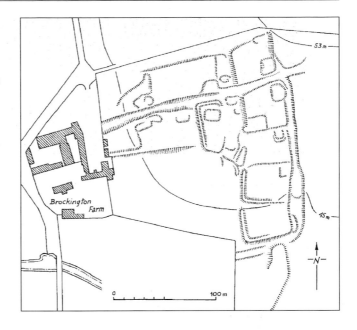

105 The deserted Medieval village of Brockington. A number of crofts (house sites) can be seen set within their own tofts (garden enclosures). After RCHME Dorset Vol V 1975 (By permission of English Heritage copyright reserved)

these deserted settlements lay. The ruined church within the Neolithic henge at Knowlton **(colour plate 13)**, placed, one suspects, to weld lingering pagan beliefs into the Christian church, is an eloquent reminder of the three settlements which formerly existed in the river valley just to the north. Here the remains of the former villages of Knowlton and Brockington can be traced although the position of the third, Phillipston, has been lost. Looking at the plan of Brockington **(105)** a sunken way or street clearly runs from the south-west to the north-east where a side street branches south-east. Following this down, a number of rectangular enclosures or tofts are visible. Within each of these are small sunken platforms upon which were constructed the crofts or simple dwellings. Occasionally, even where areas are extensively ploughed, traces of the tofts can be seen from the air with the sites of some crofts visible as distinct spreads of large flint nodules within the ploughsoil.

Other present-day villages sometimes reveal earthworks outside their current limits testifying to a time when these habitations were more extensive. Just such an area was uncovered during housing development in the 1980s at Sixpenny Handley (Sparey-Green 1996). Here, during rescue excavations, traces of postholed buildings were uncovered associated with pottery of late Saxon/early Medieval date. It is only by closely monitoring such development that we will be able to get a clearer understanding of the evolution of our village settlements.

Creation of the Chase

In Saxon times the Manor of Cranborne was part of a much larger estate known as 'The Honour of Gloucester'. It was owned by one Brictric who upon the Norman conquest was dispossessed and the lands passed into Royal ownership. An Earldom was created to go with these lands and when King John acquired the title of the Earl of Gloucester he ordered a definition, termed a 'perambulation', of the boundaries of a Chase. It became a

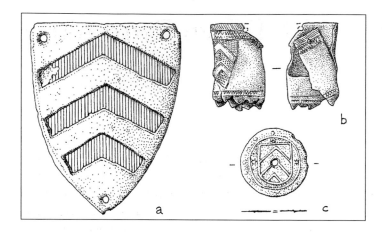

106 Medieval artefacts bearing the Arms of the de Clares, former Lords of Cranborne Chase. Dating to before 1320 AD the items consist of an enamelled mount a, a chape from a sheath b, and a jetton or reckoning counter

hunting forest reserved for the King or one of his subjects and governed by strict laws centred upon Cranborne. King John was to reside on hunting expeditions, although there is no evidence he stayed at Tollard Royal. Here, the fine Medieval building known as 'King John's House' was shown to date from a slightly later period during the excavations by General Pitt Rivers.

After the death of King John's first wife the lands and title were transferred to her sister, Amicia, who married Richard de Clare, Earl of Hertford. His son Gilbert de Clare took the titles of both his parents and became Earl of Gloucester and Hertford, although subsequent heirs were known only as the Earls of Gloucester. A document from 1280 records a dispute between King Edward I and Gilbert de Clare concerning the alleged illegal extension of the Chases' western boundary. However, de Clare was able to quote the perambulation ordered by King John and successfully refuted the claims. Remarkably, a few artefacts have been found in the area which bear the arms of the de Clares (three red chevrons on a gold background) dating from their main period of influence in the thirteenth century **(106).** The last male heir was killed at the battle of Bannockburn in 1314 and the title was transferred to one of his sisters and beyond the realms of this brief summary of the later history of the Chase.

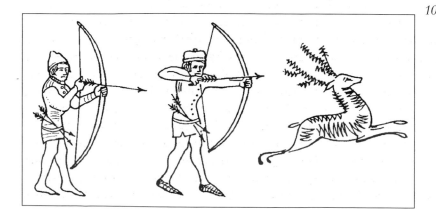

107 Medieval hunting scene. The deer is based on an engraved design taken from a button found at Gussage St.Michael (D. Bennett)

10 Down Farm today

Our farm was purchased by my grandfather in 1931 during the depression when land prices dropped to as little as £5 per acre. Farming then near Shaftesbury he had seen the opportunity to expand his business, which was supported by his two sons. Consisting then of some 366 acres (148ha) it was in a poor state with no fencing or water supply and scarred in areas of the valley floor by shallow gravel diggings. The former owner had derived most of his income from this activity by selling the gravel to the Council for road mending. In some areas only large flints marked the farm boundary. Taken over by my father in 1933 he was only just able to keep his head above water until economic conditions improved for farmers with the outbreak of war. All farms were inspected to insure they were being run efficiently and wartime legislation gave powers to remove incompetent farmers. The inspector sent to Down Farm was able to report back that it was the most improved farm he had had the pleasure of visiting. My father operated a rotational cropping programme with two years wheat, two years barley and two years grass. Grazing was at first with cattle and sheep but then later with cattle alone.

Other enterprises with pigs and chicken were gradually phased out as greater concentration was paid to the increasingly profitable cereal crops. The chickens' demise had an unexpected bonus for me, as I was able to take over their former house as my museum! By the end of the 1970s the last remaining cattle were removed and production centred entirely on cereals.

During the 1980s I became increasingly disaffected with producing cereal crops by intensive application of chemicals, although then it seemed to be the only profitable way forward. Along with archaeology I had long been interested in wildlife and conservation and was saddened to see the general reduction in the former mosaic of habitats through the latest intensive farming systems. Although it is probably necessary to have some land farmed in this way I felt that smaller units such as mine should be given the opportunity, through incentives, to farm less intensively or even recreate some of the dwindling variety of habitats. Fortunately the Ministry of Agriculture (MAFF) recognised the combined problems of over-production and decline of diversity in the British countryside, and during 1988 the Set-aside scheme was introduced. Principally designed to cut the over-production of cereal crops, its introduction may also have been influenced by the growing public awareness of conservation issues. The voluntary option of this scheme gave farmers like me the opportunity to create valuable wildlife habitats and to cease chemical farming.

That first summer in 1989 saw the farm ablaze with colour **(colour plate 1)** when long dormant seeds of cornfield annuals were given the chance to germinate. For the first time ever I was able to gaze upon such plants as corn marigold, prickly poppy and Venus' looking glass. Some seeds, however, such as the delicate corn cockle, which my father

*108   Young kestrels
in a nest box
provided at
Down Farm*

could remember as a common cornfield 'weed' before the war, had been unable to survive the long dormancy. Nevertheless, that first season's show was a heartening testimony to the resilience of nature. My main aim, however, was to manage the land in an appropriate way to encourage a gradual return to a chalk downland habitat, and to give nature a 'kick-start' I planted a grass mix which included fine fescues. Once this mix became established the cornfield annuals would not germinate until the ground was broken up again. This was not possible under Set-aside rules, but later, when part of the farm transferred to a Habitat Improvement Scheme, specific areas were ploughed annually. This not only encouraged the cornfield plants but also provided nesting areas for declining farmland birds such as lapwings and stone curlews. Systematic recording over the last decade has revealed an exciting catalogue of recolonisation by plants and animals. Downland plants have appeared in the former cereal fields including now rare species such as basil thyme and autumn gentian, and our first orchid of the pyramidal variety in 1998. One orchid may not make spotters rush to Down Farm with their cameras at the ready but it does represent the beginning of another stage in the recolonisation process.

Both insect numbers and diversity have increased dramatically and provided for a commensurate increase in small mammals and insectivorous birds. On a bright summer day the sky is alive with the song of larks, confirming the bare statistic produced by a Game Conservancy study that our former Set-aside fields are home to up to ten-times the number of species than on the surrounding intensively farmed land. The increase in 'prey' species, especially small mammals, has resulted in further colonisation by predators. Before the change to environmental management, Down Farm was home to only one breeding species of predatory bird: the kestrel (108). Now, along with these, we have regular breeding pairs of little owls, barn owls, and tawny owls. A pair of buzzards also nested in 1996 and successfully reared one chick. Foxes have bred and foraging badgers may one day take up residence. None of these species were introduced and despite the paucity of trees a few strategically placed nest boxes have been readily accepted. This goes to show that the most important factor in recolonisation is suitable habitat providing plenty of food.

During 1998 the farm joined the Countryside Stewardship Scheme which will enable further environmental benefits to accrue. A range of grassland will be maintained by sheep grazing and late hay cutting, with some areas planted for valuable scrub. Also, additional areas are to be annually cultivated to encourage further cornfield annuals and ground nesting birds. A field pond, 'seed bank' where specific seed rich plants will provide winter food for birds such as finches and buntings, and bare scraped areas are planned in the near future to increase the biological richness. The most visually interesting area of the farm archaeologically, Wyke Down, now has public access. A trail in this area incorporates burial mounds, henges, site of a Neolithic building, and parts of the Dorset Cursus and Ackling Dyke Roman road (**109**). The farm is particularly well suited to provide an educational service with its rich archaeological and environmental resources, and proposals are presently being considered to convert a former late-Victorian stable into a visitor/education centre.

109   Down Farm Countryside Stewardship Trail

The existing museum that I have painstakingly built up over the last 30 years focuses on three main themes: archaeology, local history and geology. The archaeological finds gleaned from such a small localised area, including many from the farm itself, present a picture of a landscape altered by people to meet their changing needs over time. Thanks to the exceptionally detailed work undertaken on Down Farm and described in chapter 3, its changing past ancient landscapes are very well known. It is because such a small area has been studied in such detail that the resulting information is of a much higher resolution than usual and provides an excellent model for projects studying similar landscapes. Serious scientific monitoring planned for next year, and then hopefully indefinitely, will continue these studies by looking at the vegetational and faunal changes taking place both now and in the future.

Down Farm has a continuing important role to play in furthering the knowledge of an increasingly environmentally and historically aware public.

Places to visit

Principal Museums holding Cranborne Chase material

- Salisbury & S. Wiltshire Museum — contains the Pitt Rivers Cranborne Chase collection, part of which is displayed in a gallery devoted to his life and work

- Dorset County Museum — includes on display material from the important Iron Age site at Gussage All Saints

- Priest's House Museum, Wimborne — includes Beaker and Roman finds from Barton Hill villa, Tarrant Hinton

- Red House Museum, Christchurch

- Devizes Museum — includes Colt Hoares' finds from the barrows on Oakley Down

- Rockbourne Villa Museum — see under sites

Sites

Those without public access are marked ★ and permission to visit should be sought from the respective landowners

Neolithic
- Hambledon Hill ST848122 — part of the main causewayed enclosure survives together with a fine long barrow within the hillfort

- Pimperne Long Barrow ST917104 — one of the longest in Dorset

- The Dorset Cursus — very little of this great monument survives to be seen from the ground except the SW terminal ST969124. A length of the southern bank can be seen preserved in a fence line west of the B3081 at SU018159. Walk north from here along the track which runs alongside the road and good views can be obtained of part of its course. To the west as it descends from Gussage Down, where it incorporated one of the two long barrows and to the east where it enters the Salisbury Plantation. In winter you stand a fair chance of seeing the ditches visible as soil marks from this vantage point. The NE terminal is ploughed flat but the adjacent long barrows can be seen by climbing on to Bokerley Dyke at SU041193

- Wyke Down Henge SU006152 — a short walk from the minor road to this restored henge.

- Knowlton Circles, Church & Great Barrow SU024l 02. Henges and Round Mound. Only the centre henge with the ruined Norman church is preserved and under English Heritage guardianship. The nearby Great Barrow is the largest round barrow in Dorset

- Kit's Grave Long Barrow SU035204

- Knap & Grans Barrows, Long Barrows SU089198

- Duck's Nest Long Barrow SU104203

Bronze Age
- Oakley Down Barrow Cemetery ★ (Cranborne Estate) SU018172 The finest group of barrows on Cranborne Chase

- Marleycombe Hill Barrows SU023225. Six bowl barrows in two groups of three crest this fine piece of downland. Part of an undated enclosure lies to the south of the mounds

- Martin Down Enclosure & Grim's Ditch SU042200. Excavated and restored by Pitt Rivers this enclosure probably bounded a settlement. Parts of the Grim's Ditch complex can be traced across the down, particularly clear at SU048198 where it passes two bowl barrows and on Blagdon Hill SU005180 where there are further mounds

- South Lodge Enclosure and Barrows★ (Rushmore Estate) ST954174. A settlement enclosure and contemporary barrow cemetery excavated by Pitt Rivers and re-examined in 1977-82

Iron Age & Roman
- Badbury Rings Hill Fort ST964030. Under National Trust Guardianship

- Hod Hill Fort ST856106. Under National Trust Guardianship

- Hambledon Hill Fort ST845125

- Berwick Down settlement ST941195

- Rotherley settlement ST949194

- Winkelbury Hill Fort ST951217

- Woodcutts settlement★ (Rushmore Estate) ST962181 Approach from hamlet at ST970173

- Ackling Dyke Roman Road. The best preserved stretch lies between Gussage Down SU003135 and just north of Oakley Down SU022171

- Gussage Down settlement ST995137 Although extensively ploughed, enough above ground archaeology remains to make this site worthy of visiting. The surviving monuments include lengths of multiple ditches, two long barrows and three round barrows.

- Clearbury Ring Hill Fort SU152244

- Penbury Knoll Hill Fort SU039171 This small fort has a well preserved field system below it on the north and western sides where a bowl barrow is incorporated in one field. From the fort it is only a short walk to Blagdon Hill:-

- Bokerley Dyke. This great boundary earthwork is best viewed from Blagdon Hill SU055180 and can be walked as far as Bokerley Junction SU032198

- Rockbourne Roman Villa SU120170 Opening times- April-June and September, Mon-Fri 12 noon- 6pm, Sat/Sun 10.30am-6pm. July/August 10.30am-6.30pm.

- Tidpit settlement SU070181

- Fontmell Down cross dykes ST881182, National Trust Guardianship. Well worth visiting for the view alone.

Historic Garden
- The Larmer Tree Grounds, Tollard Royal. General Pitt Rivers former pleasure grounds have recently re-opened. Opening times, Easter – end Oct 11am – 6pm daily, except Sat and special events. Tel: 01725 516228

References

Abbreviations:
PDNHAS = *Proceedings of the Dorset Natural History and Archaeological Society*
PPS = *Proceedings of the Prehistoric Society*
RCHME = *Royal Commission on Historic Monuments England*

Allen, M.J., 1997. 'Environment and land-use: the economic development of the communities who built Stonehenge (an economy to support the stones)', in B.W.Cunliffe, and A.C. Renfrew (eds), *Science and Stonehenge*, Proceedings of the British Academy 92, 115-144.

Allen, M.J., 1998 'A note on restructuring the prehistoric landscape environment in Cranborne Chase; the Allen Valley', *PDNHAS* 120, 39-44.

Allen, M.J. and M. Green, 1998. 'The Fir Tree Field Shaft; the Date and Archaeological and Paleo-Environmental Potential of a Chalk Swallowhole Feature'. *PDNHAS* 120, 25-37.

Arnold, J., M. Green, B. Lewis and R. Bradley, 1988. 'The Mesolithic of Cranborne Chase'. *PDNHAS* 110, 117-25.

Atkinson, R.J.C., J.W. Brailsford and H.G. Wakefield, 1951. 'A pond barrow at Winterbourne Steepleton, Dorset', *Archaeological Journal* 108, 1-24.

Atkinson, R.J.C., 1955. 'The Dorset Cursus', *Antiquity* 29,4-9.

Barrett, J.C., R. Bradley and M. Green, 1991. *Landscape, Monuments and Society: the prehistory of Cranborne Chase* Cambridge University Press.

Barrett, J.C., R. Bradley and M. Hall, (eds) 1991a. 'Papers on the Prehistoric Archaeology of Cranborne Chase' *Oxbow Monograph* 11.

Barton, R.N.E. and C.A. Bergman, 1982. 'Hunters at Hengistbury: some evidence from experimental archaeology' *World Archaeology* 14, 237-248.

Bersu, G. 1940. 'Excavations at Little Woodbury, Wilts; part 1' *PPS* 6, 30-111.

Bonney, D. 1961. 'Notes on excavations, 1960' *PPS* XXVII, 344.

Bowden, M. 1991. *Pitt Rivers: The life and archaeological work of Lieutenant-General Augustus Henry Lane Fox Pitt Rivers, DCL, FRS, FSA* Cambridge University Press.

Bowen, H.C. 1990. *The Archaeology of Bokerley Dyke*. London HMSO.

Bradley, R. 1986. 'The Dorset Cursus: The Archaeology of the Enigmatic', Wessex Lecture III. CBA Group 12.

Bradley, R., R. Cleal, J. Gardiner, A. Legge, F. Raymond and J. Thomas, 1984. 'Sample excavation on the Dorset Cursus ,1984 - preliminary report' *PDNHAS* 106, 128-132.

Bradley, R. and R. Entwistle, 1985. 'Thickthorn Down long barrow - a new assessment' *PDNHAS* 107, 174-6.

Brailsford, J.W. 1962. *Hod Hill Volume 1: Antiquities from the Durden Collection*, Trustees of the British Museum.

Burrow, S. and J. Gale, 1995. 'Survey and excavation at Knowlton Rings, Woodlands parish, Dorset 1993-5', *PDNHAS* 117, 131-2.

Case, H.J. 1952. 'The excavation of two round barrows at Poole, Dorset' *PPS* 18, 148-59.

Catt, J.A., M. Green and N.J. Arnold, 1980. 'Naleds in a Wessex Downland Valley', *PDNHAS* 102, 69-75.

Clay, R.C.C. 1927. 'The Woodminton group of barrows, Bowerchalke', *Wiltshire Archaeological and Natural History Magazine* 43, 313-24.

Cleal, R. and A. MacSween (eds) 1999. *Grooved Ware in Britain and Ireland*. Neolithic Studies Group Seminar Papers 3. Oxbow Books.

Colt Hoare, R. 1812. *The Ancient History of South Wiltshire* London: William Millar.

Colt Hoare, R. 1819. *The Ancient History of North Wiltshire* London: Lackington, Hughes, Harding, Mayor and Jones.

Corney, M. and M. Green., 1987. 'Recent Romano-British discoveries in the Gussage Valley' *PDNHAS* 109, 133-4.

Crawford, O.G.S. and A. Keiller, 1928. *Wessex from the Air* Oxford University Press.

Cunliffe, B. 1978. *Hengistbury Head*. London: Paul Elek.

Cunliffe, B. 1993. *Wessex to A.D. 1000*. Longman.

Darvill, T. and J. Thomas, (eds) 1996. 'Neolithic Houses in Northwest Europe and Beyond'. *Neolithic Studies Group Seminar Papers 1. Oxbow Monograph* 57.

Drew, C. and S. Piggott, 1936. 'The excavation of long barrow l63a on Thickthorn Down, Dorset' *PPS* 41, 77-96.

Drower, M. 1994. 'A visit to General Pitt Rivers'. *Antiquity* 68, number 260, 627-30.

Ellison, A., 1980a. 'Deverel-Rimbury urn cemeteries: the evidence for social organisation', in J.C. Barrett and R. Bradley (eds) *Settlement and Society in the British Later Bronze Age*, 115-26. Oxford: British Archaeological Reports, BAR 83.

Ellison, A., l980b. 'Settlements and regional exchange: a case study' in J.C. Barrett and R. Bradley (eds) *Settlement and Society in the British Later Bronze Age*, 127-40. Oxford: British Archaeological Reports, BAR 83.

Entwistle, R. and M. Bowden, 1991. 'Cranborne Chase; the molluscan evidence', in J.C. Barrett, R. Bradley and M. Hall (eds), *Papers on the Prehistoric Archaeology of Cranborne Chase*. Oxford, Oxbow Monograph 11, 1-10.

Evans, C. and M. Knight, 1996. *An Ouse-Side Longhouse - Barleycroft Farm, Cambridgeshire*. PAST 23 - newsletter of the Prehistoric Society.

Evans, J. G. and H. Jones, 1979. 'Mount Pleasant and Woodhenge: The land Mollusca', in G.J. Wainwright. 'Mount Pleasant, Dorset: Excavations 1970-71'. London, Society of Antiquaries Research Report 37, 190-213.

Feachem, R.W., 1971. 'Unfinished HillForts', in M.Jesson and D.Hill (eds) *The Iron Age and its HillForts*, 19-39, Southampton University

Field, N.H., 1962. 'Discoveries at the Knowlton Circles, Woodlands, Dorset'. *PDNHAS* 117-24.

Gardiner, J. 1984. 'Lithic distributions and Neolithic settlement patterns in central southern England', in R. Bradley and J. Gardiner (eds) *Neolithic Studies*, 15-40. British Archaeological Reports, BAR 133.

Gibson, A., 1998. *Stonehenge and Timber Circles*. Tempus.

Giles, A.G., 1981. 'Interim report on the excavations at Barton Field, Tarrant Hinton,1981'. *PDNHAS* 103, 124-5.

Green, M.T., 1985. 'Excavations in Home Field, Down Farm, Gussage St Michael'. *PDNHAS* 108, 171-3.

Green, M. and M.J. Allen, 1997. 'An Early Prehistoric Shaft on Cranborne Chase'. *Oxford Journal of Archaeology* 16, No 2, 12 1-32.

Green, M., R.N.E. Barton, N. Debenham and C.A.I. French, 1998. 'A new late-glacial open-air site at Deer Park Farm, Wimborne St.Giles, Dorset'. *PDNHAS* 120, 85-88.

Grinsell, L.V., 1959. *Dorset Barrows*. Dorset Natural History and Archaeological Society. Longmans (Dorchester).

Grinsell, L.V., 1982. *Dorset Barrows Supplement* Dorset Natural History and Archaeological Society.

Harding, D.W., I.M. Blake and P.J. Reynolds 1993. *An Iron Age settlement in Dorset Excavation and Reconstruction*. University of Edinburgh, Monograph Series No 1.

Hawkes, C.F.C. and S. Piggott, 1947. 'Britons, Romans and Saxons round Salisbury and in Cranborne Chase'. *Archaeological Journal*, 104,27-81.

Hawkins, D., 1980. *Cranborne Chase*. Victor Gollancz Ltd. London.

Higgs, E.S., 1959. 'The excavation of a late Mesolithic site at Downton, near Salisbury, Wilts.' *PPS* 25, 209-32.

Hutchins, J., 1868. *The History and Antiquities of the County of Dorset. Volume III*. Westminster: John Bowyer Nichols and Sons.

Keen, J., 1996. *A teacher's guide to Ancient Technology*. English Heritage.

Keen, L., 1976. 'Dorset Archaeology in 1976, Tarrant Hinton'. *PDNHAS* 98, 61-2.

Lewis, B. and R. Coleman, 1982. Pentridge Hill, Dorset: Trial Excavation. *PDNHAS* 104, 59-65.

Mellars, P.A., 1976. 'Settlement patterns and industrial variability in the British Mesolithic' in Sieveking, G. de G., I.H. Longworth and K.E. Wilson (eds), *Problems in Social and Economic Archaeology*. London, Duckworth, 37 5-99.

Mercer, R.J., 1980. *Hambledon Hill a Neolithic Landscape*. Edinburgh University Press.

Mercer, R.J., 1984. 'Everley Water Meadow, Iwerne Stepleton, Dorset'. *PDNHAS* 106, 110-11.

Papworth, M., 1994. 'Magnetometry Survey, Shapwick Romano-British Settlement'. *PDNHAS* 116, 131-32.

Penny, A and J.Wood, 1973. 'The Dorset Cursus complex - a Neolithic Astronomical Observatory?' *Archaeological Journal* 130,44-76.

Piggott, C.M., 1944. 'The Grim's Ditch Complex in Cranborne Chase'. *Antiquity* XVIII, 65-71.

Piggott, S., 1938. 'The Early Bronze Age in Wessex'. *PPS* 4, 52-106.

Piggott, S., 1974. *The Druids*. Penguin.

Pitt Rivers, A.H.L.F., 1884. *Report on the excavations in the Pen Pits, near Penselwood, Somerset* London: Harrison and Sons.

Pitt Rivers, A.H.L.F., 1887. *Excavations in Cranborne Chase near Rushmore on the borders of Dorset and Wiltshire. Volume I. Excavations in the Romano-British village on Woodcutts Common and Romano-British antiquities in Rushmore Park*. London (privately printed).

Pitt Rivers, A.H.L.F., 1888. *Excavations in Cranborne Chase near Rushmore on the borders of Dorset and Wiltshire 1880 - 88. Volume II. Excavations in barrows near Rushmore. Excavations in Romano-British village Rotherley. Excavations in Winkelbury Camp Excavations in British Barrows and Anglo-Saxon cemetery, Winkelbury Hill*. London (privately printed).

Pitt Rivers, A.H.L.F., 1892. *Excavations in Bokerly and Wansdyke, Dorset and Wiltshire 1888 - 91, with observations on human remains. Volume III*. London: (privately printed).

Pitt Rivers, A.H.L.F., 1898. *Excavations in Cranborne Chase near Rushmore on the borders of Dorset and Wiltshire 1893 - 1896. Volume IV. South Lodge Camp, Rushmore Park. Handley Hill Entrenchment. Stone Age and Bronze Age Barrows and Camp, Handley, Dorset Martin Down Camp & c*. London (privately printed).

Pollard, J., 1995. 'The Durrington 68 timber circle: a forgotten late Neolithic monument'. *Wiltshire Archaeological and Natural History Magazine*, 88, 122-126.

Reid, C., 1915. 'Excavations at Dewlish'. *PDNHAS* XXXVI , 209-24.

Richards, J., 1999. *Meet The Ancestors*. BBC.

Richmond, I., 1968. *Hod Hill. Vol.2 Excavations carried out between 1951-58*. London: British Museum.

RCHM, 1972. *County of Dorset, Volume 4, North*. London: HMSO.

RCHM 1975. *County of Dorset, Volume 5, East*. London: HMSO.

RCHM 1983. 'West Park Roman Villa, Rockbourne'. *Archaeological Journal* 140,129-50.

Selkirk, A., (ed) 1980. *Current Archaeology* 74.

Sparey-Green, C., 1997. 'Excavations at the Town Farm House Site, now The Orchard, Dean Lane, Sixpenny Handley', 1988. *PDNHAS* 119, 87-102.

Sparey-Green, C., 1998. 'Interim Report on Excavations at Myncen Farm, Sixpenny Handley, Dorset' *PDNHAS* 120, 91-4.

Speake, G., 1989. 'A Saxon Bed Burial on Swallowcliffe Down'. London: English Heritage Archaeological Report 10.

Stone, J.F.S., 1931. 'Easton Down, Winterslow, S. Wilts, Flint Mine Excavation 1930'. Wiltshire Archaeological and Natural History Magazine Vol XIV No. CLIV, 35 0-65.

Stone, J.F.S., 1931. A Settlement Site of the Beaker Period on Easton Down, Winterslow, S.Wilts. Wiltshire Archaeological and Natural History Magazine Vol XIV No. CLIV, 366-7 2.

Summers, P.G., 1941. 'A Mesolithic site, near Iwerne Minster, Dorset'. *PPS* 7, notes 145-6.

Sumner, H, 1913. *The Ancient Earthworks of Cranborne Chase*. London: Chiswick Press.

Sumner, H, 1914. *Excavations on Rockbourne Down, Hampshire*. London: Chiswick Press.

Taylor, C.C., 1970. *Dorset*. London.

Thompson, M.W., 1977. *General Pitt Rivers: Evolution and Archaeology in the Nineteenth Century*. Moonraker Press. Bradford-on-Avon.

Tilley, C., 1994. *A Phenomenology of Landscape*. Oxford: Berg.

Toms, H.S., 1925. 'Bronze Age or earlier lynchets'. *PDNHAS* 46, 89-100.

Wainwright, G.W., 1968. 'The excavation of a Durotrigian farmstead near Tollard Royal, in Cranborne Chase, Southern England'. *PPS* 34, 102-47.

Wainwright, G.W. (ed), 1979. 'Gussage All Saints. An Iron Age Settlement in Dorset'. *DOE Archaeological Reports* 10. London HMSO.

Wainwright, G.W. and I.H. Longworth. 1971. *Durrington Walls: Excavations 1966-68*. London: Society of Antiquaries.

Warne, C., 1866. *The Celtic Tumuli of Dorset: an account of personal and other researches in the sepulchral mounds of the Durotriges*. London: John Russell Smith.

Warne, C., 1872. *Ancient Dorset: the Celtic, Roman, Saxon, and Danish antiquities of the County*. Privately Printed.

White, D.A., 1970. 'Excavation of an Iron Age round barrow near Handley, Dorset, 1969'. *Antiquaries Journal*, 50, 26-36.

Glossary

Aceramic phases in which pottery was no longer used or produced

Agger raised causeway or embankment upon which Roman roads are sometimes constructed

Ballista a small Roman artillery weapon resembling a large crossbow, stretched with sinew and capable of firing showers of arrows over considerable distances

Counter-scarp a low bank on the outside of a ditch, resulting from regular maintenance of the ditch, which incidentally produces an additional obstacle

Deverel-Rimbury the name given to the Middle Bronze Age pottery styles prevalent in the Wessex region. Named after two cemeteries excavated in Dorset in the nineteenth century which produced large numbers of urns

Doline a closed hollow or depression in a chalk landscape, formed by the solution of chalk or limestone near the surface, and subsequent subsidence. Often round or elliptical on the surface

Glacis a glacis rampart represents a continuous unbroken slope which continues the same line as the underlying ditch side

Horizon (archaeological use) an occupation level within sediments
(soil) a layer within a soil which lies more or less parallel to the surface. It is distinguished by fairly distinct physical and chemical properties and often characterises the processes that have created it or the type of soil

Loess coarse grained wind-blown deposits or dust originating in cold dry (periglacial) conditions. In southern Britain it deposition is largely attributed to a part of the Middle Devensian c.30,000-14,000BP. Many soils in southern Britain therefore have a loessic component

Oppidum imprecise term used to refer to large settlements of town-like proportions

Periglacial the zone around and next to the glacier. It generally refers to an area with an arctic or subarctic climate

Naled ice bodies typically formed in periglacial conditions where springs issue from the ground. Subsequent melting often leaves a characteristic series of mounds and hollows

Rendzina a thin soil with no horizons, typically formed under grass on chalk and lime-rich rocks, which rests directly upon the underlying natural geology

Rod a particular type of microlith consisting of narrow needle-like points blunted on one or both ends by retouch. Particularly prevalent in the later Mesolithic

Toft the property boundary, often rectilinear, within which is located a croft (dwelling). Today, deserted village sites are often visible as a series of these enclosures

Tranchet a term used to describe both a technical act and, by extension, several types of stone artefact. In essence, a tranchet blow is one delivered close to the cutting edge of a tool and at 90 degrees to its long axis. Usually associated with the creation of cutting edges on so-called 'tranchet blow' axes, the term is also used to describe axes made of large flakes where the cutting edge is formed by the side of the original flake, although strictly these should be termed 'pseudo-tranchet'

Radiocarbon graphs and tables

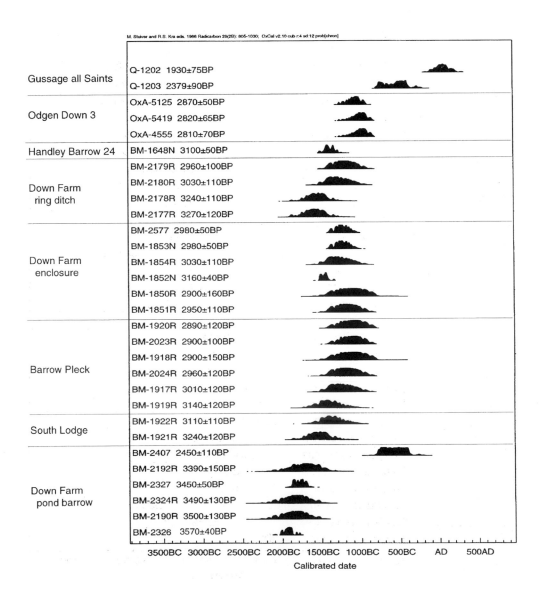

M. Stuiver and R.S. Kra eds. 1986 Radiocarbon 28(2B): 805–1030; OxCal v2.10 cub r:4 sd:12 prob[chron]

Gussage all Saints	Q-1202 1930±75BP
	Q-1203 2379±90BP
Odgen Down 3	OxA-5125 2870±50BP
	OxA-5419 2820±65BP
	OxA-4555 2810±70BP
Handley Barrow 24	BM-1648N 3100±50BP
Down Farm ring ditch	BM-2179R 2960±100BP
	BM-2180R 3030±110BP
	BM-2178R 3240±110BP
	BM-2177R 3270±120BP
Down Farm enclosure	BM-2577 2980±50BP
	BM-1853N 2980±50BP
	BM-1854R 3030±110BP
	BM-1852N 3160±40BP
	BM-1850R 2900±160BP
	BM-1851R 2950±110BP
Barrow Pleck	BM-1920R 2890±120BP
	BM-2023R 2900±100BP
	BM-1918R 2900±150BP
	BM-2024R 2960±120BP
	BM-1917R 3010±120BP
	BM-1919R 3140±120BP
South Lodge	BM-1922R 3110±110BP
	BM-1921R 3240±120BP
Down Farm pond barrow	BM-2407 2450±110BP
	BM-2192R 3390±150BP
	BM-2327 3450±50BP
	BM-2324R 3490±130BP
	BM-2190R 3500±130BP
	BM-2326 3570±40BP

3500BC 3000BC 2500BC 2000BC 1500BC 1000BC 500BC AD 500AD

Calibrated date

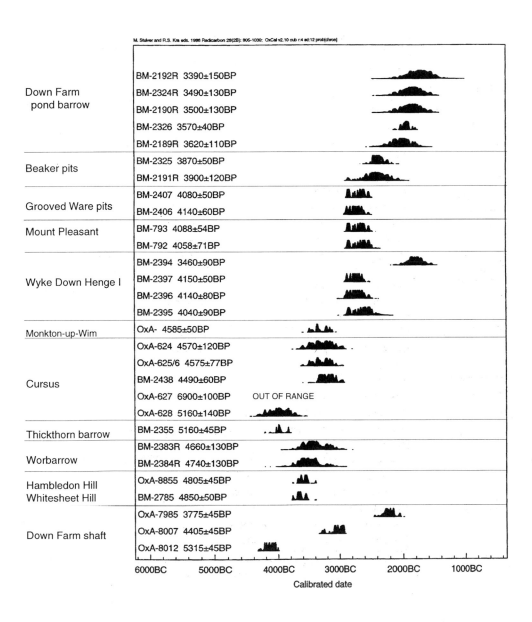

M. Stuiver and R.S. Kra eds. 1986 Radiocarbon 28(2B): 805-1030; OxCal v2.10 cub r:4 sd:12 prob[chron]

Down Farm pond barrow	BM-2192R 3390±150BP	
	BM-2324R 3490±130BP	
	BM-2190R 3500±130BP	
	BM-2326 3570±40BP	
	BM-2189R 3620±110BP	
Beaker pits	BM-2325 3870±50BP	
	BM-2191R 3900±120BP	
Grooved Ware pits	BM-2407 4080±50BP	
	BM-2406 4140±60BP	
Mount Pleasant	BM-793 4088±54BP	
	BM-792 4058±71BP	
Wyke Down Henge I	BM-2394 3460±90BP	
	BM-2397 4150±50BP	
	BM-2396 4140±80BP	
	BM-2395 4040±90BP	
Monkton-up-Wim	OxA- 4585±50BP	
Cursus	OxA-624 4570±120BP	
	OxA-625/6 4575±77BP	
	BM-2438 4490±60BP	
	OxA-627 6900±100BP	OUT OF RANGE
	OxA-628 5160±140BP	
Thickthorn barrow	BM-2355 5160±45BP	
Worbarrow	BM-2383R 4660±130BP	
	BM-2384R 4740±130BP	
Hambledon Hill Whitesheet Hill	OxA-8855 4805±45BP	
	BM-2785 4850±50BP	
Down Farm shaft	OxA-7985 3775±45BP	
	OxA-8007 4405±45BP	
	OxA-8012 5315±45BP	

6000BC   5000BC   4000BC   3000BC   2000BC   1000BC

Calibrated date

Location	material	lab ref	determination	cal BC (2 sig)
FIRTREE FIELD SHAFT				
Main Shaft Fill				
-3.50m (sample 15), below lens 1	*Corylus*	OxA-8012	5315 ± 45 BP	4330 - 4000
Weathering Cone				
L5 (sample 3) Turf with Peterb only	*Corylus* charcoal	OxA-8007	4405 ± 45 BP	3310 - 2910
L2a (sample 1) Beaker chalk dump	Pig femur	OxA-7985	3775 ± 45 BP	2460 - 2040
WHITESHEET HILL				
enclosure ditch, bottom	Bone	BM-2785	4850 ± 50 BP	3780 - 3380
HAMBLEDON HILL				
enclosure ditch, bottom	Animal bone	OxA-8855	4805 ± 45 BP	3660 - 3380
WOR BARROW				
long barrow ditch, bottom	Antler	BM-2284R	4740 ± 130 BP	3790 - 3100
long barrow ditch, primary fill	Antler	BM-2283R	4660 ± 130 BP	3780 - 2940
THICKTHORN DOWN				
Surface of buried soil under barrow	Animal bone	BM-2355	5160 ± 45 BP	4040 - 3810
DORSET CURSUS Chalkpit Field				
primary silts	Animal bone	OxA-628*	6460 ± 140 BP	5640 - 5140
primary silts, surface of primary	Animal bone	OxA-627*	6900 ± 100 BP	5980 - 5560
primary silts, surface of primary	Animal bone	BM-2438	4490 ± 60 BP	3370 - 2920
secondary silts - lower silts	Animal bone	OxA-625/6	4575 ± 77 BP	3520 - 3040
secondary silts - middle of silts	Animal bone	OxA-624	4570 ± 120 BP	3640 - 2920
MONKTON-UP-WIMBORNE				
Burial group	Human bone	OxA-8035	4585 ± 50 BP	3500 - 3100
Flexed burial (Adam)	Human bone	OxA-8034	3180 ± 40 BP	1530 - 1400
WYKE DOWN				
Pit I – primary fill	Antler	BM-2395	4040 ± 90 BP	2890 - 2480
Pit I – recut	Charcoal (oak hw)	BM-2396	4140 ± 80 BP	2920 - 2490
Pit K – recut	Charcoal	BM-2397	4150 ± 50 BP	2900 - 2580
central pit	Animal bone	BM-2394	3460 ± 90 BP	2030 - 1530
MOUNT PLEASANT HENGE				
Ditch primary fill (11) north entrance	Charcoal *Quercus*	BM-792	4058 ± 71 BP	2890 - 2460
Ditch primary fill (12) north entrance	Charcoal *Quercus*	BM-793	4088 ± 54 BP	2870 - 2470
DOWN FARM (FTF 78) - Grooved Ware Pits				
Pit 11a	Antler	BM-2406	4140 ± 60 BP	2910 - 2500
Pit 32	Antler	BM-2407	4080 ± 50 BP	2880 - 2490
KNOWLTON CIRCLE (southern)				
Ditch	Charcoal	Beta 141096	3890 ± 60 BP	2570 - 2190
DOWN FARM (FTF 81) Beaker Pits				
Feature 28	Charcoal (oak hw)	BM-2191R	3900 ± 120 BP	2870 - 2040
Feature 31	Charcoal (oak hw)	BM-2325	3870 ± 50 BP	2490 - 2140
DOWN FARM (FTF 81) Pond Barrow				
Feature 2	Charcoal (oak hw)	BM- 2189R	3620 ± 110 BP	2320 - 1690
Feature 3	Charcoal (yw)	BM- 2326	3570 ± 40 BP	2040 - 1780
Feature 12	Charcoal (yw)	BM-2190R	3500 ± 130 BP	2200 - 1520
Feature 30, upper fill	Charcoal (yw)	BM-2324R	3490 ± 130 BP	2200 - 1520
Posthole 8	Charcoal (yw)	BM-2327	3450 ± 50 BP	1900 - 1670
Posthole 10	Charcoal (yw)	BM-2192R	3390 ± 150 BP	2140 - 1400
Posthole 12	Animal bone	BM-2407	2450 ± 110 BP	920 – 400
SOUTH LODGE CAMP				
Posthole A529	Charcoal	BM-1921R	3240 ± 120 BP	1880 - 3200
Posthole A529 (2nd sample)	Charcoal	BM-1922R	3110 ± 110 BP	1630 - 1050

Location	material	lab ref	determination	cal BC (2 sig)
BARROW PLECK				
Cremation BPA 011	Charcoal	BM-1919R	3140 ± 120 BP	1690 - 1090
Cremation BPA 005	Charcoal	BM-1917R	3010 ± 120 BP	1520 - 910
Cremation BPA 014	Charcoal	BM-2024R	2960 ± 120 BP	1510 - 840
Cremation BPA 010	Charcoal	BM-1918R	2900 ± 150 BP	1510 - 800
Cremation BPA 02301 -2nd sample	Charcoal	BM-2023R	2900 ± 100 BP	1420 - 830
Cremation BPA 02301	Charcoal	BM-1920R	2890 ± 120 BP	1420 - 810
DOWN FARM (DF 78) enclosure				
Lowest midden in enclosure ditch	Charcoal	BM-1851R	2950 ± 110 BP	1440 - 900
Middle midden in enclosure ditch	Charcoal	BM-1850R	2900 ± 160 BP	1510 - 800
Upper midden in enclosure ditch	Charcoal	BM-1852N*	3160 ± 40 BP	1520 - 1320
Upper midden in enclosure ditch	Charcoal	BM-1854R	3030 ± 110 BP	1520 - 940
Upper midden in enclosure ditch	Charcoal	BM-1853N	2980 ± 50 BP	1400 - 1040
Upper midden in enclosure ditch	Charcoal (yw)	BM-2577	2980 ± 50 BP	1400 - 1040
DOWN FARM (DF 80) ring ditch				
Top of Neolithic recut ditch	Charcoal (oak hw)	BM-2177R	3270 ± 120 BP	1880 - 1310
Flint packing from top level of ditch	Charcoal (oak hw)	BM-2178R	3240 ± 110 BP	1860 - 1260
Cremation 6	Charcoal (yw)	BM-2180R	3030 ± 110 BP	1520 - 940
Cremation 12	Charcoal (yw)	BM-2179R	2960 ± 100 BP	1430 - 910
HANDLEY BARROW 24				
Deposit 38	Charcoal	BM-1648N	3100 ± 50 BP	1510 - 1260
OGDEN DOWN (OGD 3)				
Ditch - base of recut	ave OxA-5419+4555		2810 ± 70 BP	1110 - 840
Ditch - base of recut	repeat OxA-5419	OxA-4555	2810 ± 70 BP	1220 - 820
Ditch - base of recut	Red deer antler	OxA-5419	2820 ± 65 BP	1220 - 830
Posthole 102 (inner circle)	Charcoal - oak	OxA-5125	2870 k 50 BP	1250 - 910
GUSSAGE ALL SAINTS (Iron Age enclosure)				
Pit 379	Charcoal	Q-1203	2370 ± 90 BP	790-310
Ditch 310	Charcoal	Q-1202	1930 ± 75 BP	110 -cal AD250

Index

The index entriea are arranged in letter-by-letter order. Page numbers in bold refer to tables; page numbers in italics refer to figures